MONTGOMERY COLLEGE LIBRARY
GERMANTOWN CAMPUS

GOVERNMENT BY EXPERTS

Government by Experts

THE NEXT STAGE IN POLITICAL EVOLUTION

Burnham P. Beckwith, Ph. D.

An Exposition-University Book
Exposition Press   New York

EXPOSITION PRESS, INC.
50 Jericho Turnpike, Jericho, New York 11753

FIRST EDITION

© 1972 by Burnham P. Beckwith. All rights reserved,
including the right of reproduction in whole
or in part in any form except for
short quotations in critical essays and reviews.
Manufactured in the United States of America.

LIBRARY OF CONGRESS CATALOG CARD NO.: 72-84068

SBN 0-682-47539-4

Contents

PREFACE vii
1 INTRODUCTION 3
My Thesis; The Idea of Progress; Political Democracy; Government by Experts Compared with Alternatives; Scientific Prediction and Scientific Argument.
2 A REVIEW OF RELEVANT EARLIER DOCTRINES 11
Saint Simon; The Conservative Elitists; Socialist Elitists; The Fabians; The Technocrats; The Managerialists; Santayana and Jordan; Michael Young; H. W. Eldredge; General Neglect of the Idea of Government by Experts; The Reasons for the Neglect.
3 WHY GOVERNMENT BY EXPERTS IS COMING 36
Introduction; Voters Are Incompetent; Experts Are Competent; Social Problems Become More Complex and Numerous; Declining Interest in Political Problems; Politicians Must Play Politics, Government by Experts Is Superior to Dictatorship and Monarchy; The Growth of Knowledge; The Growth and Democratization of Education; Eugenic Reform; The Equalization of Incomes; The Rise of Socialism; The High Costs of Democratic Elections; The Decline of Religion; World Government; A Summary of the Relevant Effects of Long-Run Social Trends.
4 A CRITICAL REVIEW OF THE CASE FOR POLITICAL DEMOCRACY 74
The Many Are Wiser Than the Few; Democratic Rulers Listen to the People; Democracy Reduces the Danger of Riots and Revolutions; Democracy Equalizes Political Influence; Democracy Represents All Interests; Democracy Makes Men Feel Free; Democracy Educates the Public; Democracy Makes Men More Moral; Democracy Favors the Rise of the Most Able; The Natural Rights Argument; Democracy Can Be Greatly Improved.

5	THE CHIEF ARGUMENTS AGAINST GOVERNMENT BY EXPERTS	87
	Experts Would Enrich Themselves; Expert Government Would Be Unpopular; Experts Know How, Not What; Experts Cannot Balance Competing Interests; Experts Would Impose Their Consumption Patterns; Government Work Can Be Simplified.	
6	THE CHIEF CRITICS OF GOVERNMENT BY EXPERTS	99
	George Santayana; C. A. R. Crosland; Peregrine Worsthorne; Michael Young; Bernard Crick; David Riesman; T. D. Weldon; Final Comments.	
7	THE TRANSITION TO GOVERNMENT BY EXPERTS	124
	The Transition in Democratic States—Old Trends Leading to Government by Experts: The Growth of Civil Service; The Growing Employment of City and County Managers; More Autonomy for Government Agencies; More Government Use of Legislative Experts; The Centralization of Government; More Professional Business Managers. New Trends Toward Government by Experts: Higher Educational Qualifications for Candidates; The Restriction of Legislative Work; The Rise of Professional Journalists; The Rise of Professional School Administrators; Government Financing of Political Campaigns; More Advice by Professional Associations. The Transition in Undemocratic Countries.	
8	A PLAN OF GOVERNMENT BY EXPERTS	138
	The Choice of Legislators; The Functions of the National Legislature; Agency Legislatures; The Choice of the Chief Executive; The Retention of Democratic Ritual.	
9	CONCLUSION	152
	The Logic of My Prediction; Why It Has Been Ignored; How Long Will the Transition Last?; Is Government by Experts the Ultimate Stage?	
	NOTES	157
	SELECT ANNOTATED BIBLIOGRAPHY	160
	INDEX	164

Preface

In the last ten years there has been a rapid growth of interest in scientific, non-utopian prediction of future events and social trends. The number of books in this field published during the last decade is probably larger than that published during the previous fifty years. And the first scholarly journal, *The Futurist,* was begun in 1967.

In 1967 I published one of the pioneer studies in futurism, *The Next 500 Years, Scientific Prediction of Future Social Trends.* It covers most important social trends in fifteen different major fields—industry, finance, health, education, crime, and so forth. The chapter on government has nine sections. One of them, "Government by Experts" (pp. 58-63), contains a brief statement of the thesis of this book. This thesis is so significant and original that it deserves far more space than I could give it in *The Next 500 Years.* That is why I have elaborated it in the present essay.

The great majority of recent efforts at scientific prediction have covered only the next thirty to fifty years. *The Next 500 Years* is one of the very few which attempts scientific prediction for centuries instead of decades ahead. And *Government by Experts* also covers several centuries.

Most readers will undoubtedly be skeptical of anyone's ability to make scientific predictions covering such long periods. In reply to such possible criticism, I would first emphasize that a prediction does not have to be 100 percent certain, or even 80 percent certain, to be scientific. All scientific truths are merely probable truths, and any probable truth is a scientific truth. However, I am convinced that the odds in favor of the truth of my basic thesis concerning government by experts are better than two to one.

In *The Next 500 Years,* I suggested and discussed twelve different methods of predicting the future, many more than any previous writer had proposed. Of these twelve, only six are useful in predicting the rise of government by experts, namely:

1. The projection of past trends.
2. The study of trends in expert opinion.
3. A comparison of expert and lay opinion.
5. A comparison of the most and least efficient organizations in an advanced country.
11. A study of utopias and science fiction.
12. The prediction that men will act more and more rationally.

The first and last methods are the most useful here. I believe that the long record of human progress from ape-man to Nobel Prize winner fully justifies the prediction that men will behave in an ever more rational manner in every field of problem-solving behavior.

Because I have discussed the methodology of scientific prediction of future social trends in a previous work, I shall say little about it here.

All of the social trends, other than the rise of government by experts, discussed in this book—for instance, eugenic progress and the rise of world government—are more fully treated in *The Next 500 Years.*

I am not a political scientist. I am an economist, without even a college minor in political science. I had read very little of its literature before beginning to prepare to write this essay. I first began to think about the theory of an ideal government in the early 1930s, when writing the first edition of my *Economic Theory of a Socialist Economy* (1949), which includes a one-chapter proposal or plan for a democratic socialist government. In that twenty-three-page chapter, only one brief paragraph (pp. 92-93), is devoted to a plea for greater reliance on experts in government.

Twenty-five years later, when revising this chapter for its inclusion in *Liberal Socialism* (still unpublished), I was more aware of the need for increased reliance on experts and for eventual control by experts in every economic, social, or political organization. The revised chapter on organization includes a

Preface

three-page section, "More Use of Experts," emphasizing these points and predicting the replacement of democratic government by expert government some time after the full achievement of socialism. I did not consider government by experts a prerequisite for or a part of liberal socialism, and therefore did not elaborate the idea.

As soon as I had finished writing the manuscript of *Liberal Socialism*, in late 1961, I elaborated my prediction of the rise of government by experts. I wrote a seven thousand-word article and submitted it, unsuccessfully, to various magazines. Then I became engrossed in writing *The Next 500 Years* (1967). But as, from time to time, I thought about government by experts, I became more and more convinced of the significance of the idea, and I decided to expand my 1962 article into a book as soon as I had finished *The Next 500 Years*. This present book was written in Menlo Park in the years 1967-69, and will be my final treatment of government by experts, the next stage in political evolution. I hope it will stimulate other writers to treat this significant idea more fully and more competently.

GOVERNMENT BY EXPERTS

1
Introduction

MY THESIS

I have written this book to state, elaborate, and defend the novel thesis that government by experts in government, i.e., by applied social scientists or social engineers, will be the next major stage in political evolution. In other words, I shall argue that in advanced nations the democratic form of government will be followed inevitably by government by experts. I shall not claim that democracy is a bad form of government. It is the best the world has known. Rather I shall argue that social progress will result in the rise of government by experts as a higher form of government suitable to the more advanced society of the future. This future is not remote. Within three hundred years all advanced countries, perhaps the entire world, will have largely adopted this form of government. In the meantime, democratic government will improve and spread for another century or two, but will rely more and more on the use of experts.

In chapter 7 I will predict many detailed features of the coming government by experts, partly in order to make my general prediction more meaningful. But predictions concerning details are nearly always much less certain than predictions concerning the general character of a future trend. I am very confident that some form of government by experts will follow political democracy in all mature democracies. (Immature ones may temporarily relapse into dictatorships or monarchy.) But I am much less confident that my more detailed predictions concerning the form of the coming government by experts will be confirmed.

Because these detailed predictions will be offered in a separate chapter, they require little discussion here. However, I will now summarize the most general features of the coming political system in order to help the reader understand what I mean by the term "government by experts."

The term "expert" means a person who has special skill or knowledge, but many people think of an expert as a specialist in a narrow field. *Obviously, the top legislators and executives of a nation should not be narrow specialists. They should have a very broad knowledge of social problems and considerable experience in a variety of politico-social activities.* By referring to such generalists as experts, I mean that they have had the education and experience which best qualifies them for high government office. A lawyer, or an engineer, or a salesman elected to high office at age forty or fifty may have had a professional education and a wide variety of experience, but he is not an expert in government. Only a man trained as a social scientist and with long experience in government, university teaching, or research should be considered an expert in government.

My thesis assumes that social progress and political evolution are inevitable and predictable and describes the next stage in political evolution.[1] Thus, a few comments on social progress and political evolution are in order.

THE IDEA OF PROGRESS

When social change is very slow, it is imperceptible, and it has been imperceptible throughout most of human history. As J. B. Bury has shown in his stimulating work, *The Idea of Progress,* the idea of long-run, inevitable social advance or evolution is fairly new, having been first stated in the eighteenth century and not popularized until the nineteenth. Previously, for over two thousand years, Western intellectuals and laymen had universally accepted the doctrine of the fall of man from a previous golden age or from the Garden of Eden. Even among the anticlerical philosophes, many, including Rousseau, believed that ancient Greek or Roman civilization had been superior to contemporary European civilization.

Introduction

Once the theory of progress had been clearly formulated, however, it was rapidly adopted and elaborated by advanced thinkers, who found it a powerful weapon against conservatives, as well as a vital key to the understanding of history and of current social problems. Within a century, detailed theories of geological, biological, intellectual, and social evolution were stated. Today such theories of evolution are generally accepted by educated conservatives, as well as by liberals and radicals. The basic reason for the development and ever-growing acceptance of the idea of progress is simply that the rate of change has accelerated so much that change has become not only perceptible but obvious. Few conservatives now reject the idea of continual social change; they merely question or reject the term "progress." Conservatives consider most social changes harmful, not progressive.

While theories of geological, biological, intellectual, and social revolution are all recent, the Greeks developed theories of political cycles and devolution. For instance, in the *Critias* Plato described five normally successive stages of such devolution—aristocracy, timocracy, oligarchy, democracy, and despotism. He thought of aristocracy as the ideal form of government, and the succeeding stages as steps in political degeneration. He attributed this inevitable degeneration to laxity and errors in state regulation of marriage and birth.[2]

Other Greek writers believed in a recurring political cycle—monarchy, aristocracy, democracy, dictatorship, monarchy. Observing the history of Greek city-states, they concluded that the evils of democracy usually resulted in the rise of a dictatorship, which tended to become, sooner or later, a hereditary monarchy, whose evils led first to aristocracy and then to democracy.

The modern theory that progressive social evolution through widely differing stages of political and economic development is universal and inevitable was first elaborated and popularized by Karl Marx and Frederick Engels. They stressed the major economic stages—slavery, feudalism, capitalism, socialism, and communism—but they taught that economic evolution results in corresponding political evolution.

Capitalist political scientists now accept the theory of past political evolution, but they predict no new major political stage beyond democratic government. The most popular outline of such evolution is feudal monarchy, absolute monarchy, constitutional monarchy, democracy. While political development has of course varied from country to country, this is a good general outline of normal political evolution in Western Europe since 1000 A.D. I do not propose to question or revise it here. Rather I wish to discuss in detail a grossly neglected topic, namely the inevitable next stage in political evolution after democracy. But first a few preliminary words about democractic government are in order.

POLITICAL DEMOCRACY

Democratic government is a very recent historical development, and one which has as yet become firmly established in only a few very advanced countries. The so-called democratic Greek city-states were aristocracies based upon slavery. As recently as 1860, no country had a democratic government. The United States still had millions of slaves. And "until the last quarter of the 19th century, in most of Western and Northern Europe, the proportion of voters to population was not more than 5 percent."[3] Even in 1890 only 15 percent of the American population voted (as compared with 27 percent of the French population in the 1881 election). By 1900, voters were still only 11 percent of the population in the United Kingdom: they rose to 43 percent in 1922, after women had been given the vote. In Southern and Eastern Europe democracy is non-existent or new and feeble even today. Moreover, there is no mature, firmly established democratic government anywhere in Asia or Africa. Japan, like Germany, has had democratic government forced upon it by alien conquerors, but such democracy can scarcely be considered popular or firmly established. In sum, less than 15 percent of the world's population live in countries with stable, mature, democratic governments, and these countries have been democratic for less than a century.

Introduction

The term "democracy" has been used to denote various kinds of governments. It is a popular term, and therefore many states that are clearly not democratic, as well as others that are slightly or intermittently democratic, claim to be politically democratic. The best practical test is to determine how often an opposition party has won a national election. If the opposition never wins (as in Mexico and the U.S.S.R.), the country is not politically democratic, no matter how many people vote in regular elections. And one opposition win does not prove that a country is democratic. Moreover, a country in which regular elections are held and often won by the opposition may be aristocratic or oligarchic. To be democratic a state must allow the great majority of men to vote, and must give them fairly equal representation in government. Rotten boroughs are highly undemocratic.

The democratic governments of capitalist states are, of course, only partially democratic, semi-democratic. Some have many rotten boroughs, and in all boroughs rich men have far more political influence than poor men. The rich control the radio and television stations, newspapers, and magazines, and contribute most of the political campaign funds. Nevertheless, peaceful social reform has been almost continuous in these states, and they are steadily becoming more and more democratic. How fully democratic they will become before they adopt government by experts is still uncertain. In any case, the democratic phase in political evolution is likely to be a relatively short one. It will probably last less than three hundred years in the United States, and less than a century in many states, notably those that are least advanced. Some may move directly from enlightened dictatorship to government by experts.

Much of this book is devoted to a criticism of democracy. I believe, however, that modern democratic governments are the most efficient and competent the world has ever known, and that for many years they will become more numerous and more successful in increasing human welfare. I have the greatest admiration for the long line of progressive thinkers and reformers who helped to create and popularize the ideas and institutions of democratic government. My criticism of democracy is not conservative or reactionary, but evolutionary. I criticize it solely in order to explain why and how it will gradually be replaced by an even more effective and advanced method of government, namely government by experts chosen by experts.

GOVERNMENT BY EXPERTS COMPARED WITH ALTERNATIVES

My definition of government by experts may become clearer if I compare such government with some other forms.

Government by experts is an oligarchy, in other words government by a very small minority, but it is not aristocracy because no member of the ruling minority would inherit his position or an exclusive right to seek it. Government by experts is political meritocracy, which can be only one part of a complete meritocracy. When meritocracy is complete, all leaders in all fields of activity will be chosen on the basis of their ability, not their status or popularity.

The governments of advanced states are already largely bureaucratic, and will steadily become more so. The growth of bureaucracy favors specialization and government by experts, but bureaucracy is not government by experts. A bureaucratic government may have a leader who is a king, a dictator, a democratically elected chief executive, or an expert chosen by experts.

The chief executive of a government ruled by experts would not be a dictator because he would be chosen by experts and would serve either a fixed term or at the pleasure of a large body of fellow experts. Thus, government by experts would not be dictatorial. The transfer of power from one administration to another would be as orderly and constitutional as in a democratic country.

The experts who would rule a nation under government by experts would form an elite. Such government is therefore a form of elitism. But most writers on political elites and elitism have discussed only hereditary elites and/or government by such elites. The experts who will eventually rule all nations and

Introduction

the world state will make up a non-hereditary political elite, an ever-changing group of political meritocrats.

The term "meritocracy" has been recently coined to denote a society in which the ablest rise to the top in every profession and social organization. Government by experts would enable the ablest men to achieve high political office. A nation ruled by experts would be a political meritocracy. I shall therefore sometimes use "political meritocracy" as a near synonym for "government by experts." The latter term places more emphasis on specialized scientific knowledge and experience than the former. "Political meritocracy" suggests equality of political opportunity more than "expert government" does. Political meritocracy is conceivable in a pre-scientific age, for instance in a Greek city-state. But government by experts is conceivable only in an age of advanced social science.

SCIENTIFIC PREDICTION AND SCIENTIFIC ARGUMENT

What is the difference between an argument that explains in detail why, for scientific reasons, society should adopt a major social reform, like socialism or government by experts, and a scientific prediction that society will adopt this reform? Both argument and prediction should cover virtually the same reasons, but the former concludes with *ought,* and the latter with *will.* However, the *ought* is not a moral *ought.* Both theories can be scientific.

The first and principal difference is that the prediction assumes that men usually or eventually do what will benefit them, in other words, that they are hedonistic and rational. These are not rare or absurd assumptions. Political economy, the most highly developed of all the social sciences, has long been based squarely on them. And critics of these assumptions have been unable to develop a useful alternative explanation of economic behavior. Moreover, modern realistic theories of political behavior also assume that men seek rationally to use the government to achieve personal or group political ends.

The second difference between scientific argument for and scientific prediction of social reform is that the former often ignores the question of whether social conditions and/or popular prejudices now permit or favor the reform in question. It may be objected that a scientific argument should always discuss and evaluate these factors, but few of them do so. Most arguments for social reform merely assume or imply that the reform in question is now politically feasible, as well as socially desirable.

By contrast, a scientific prediction that a social reform will be adopted normally explains why the reform is not now feasible and why predictable changes in social conditions and prejudices will eventually make it feasible. It also usually estimates how long it will be before these necessary preliminary changes have gone far enough to bring about the reform in question.

The third difference is that a scientific prediction is more easily verifiable than a scientific argument. An argument usually claims or implies that a reform will be beneficial; a prediction, only that it will be adopted. It is much easier to prove that a change has occurred than that it has increased social welfare.

In spite of these differences, it is notable that scientific arguments for social reforms and scientific predictions of such reforms are very similar. Only minor changes are required to convert an argument into a prediction, or the opposite. Thus, any reader of this book who believes that social changes cannot be predicted may take my scientific prediction of government by experts as an argument for such government. I believe that the adoption of government by experts will be beneficial, and that is the chief reason why I predict this radical reform.

2

A Review of Relevant Earlier Doctrines

My chief purpose in writing this book is to state, elaborate, and defend the prediction that expert government will be the next major stage in political evolution after democratic government, not to review and criticize earlier foreshadowings or anticipations of this theory. However, a brief review of relevant earlier doctrines should help the reader to determine how novel and significant my prediction is.

The theory that expert government will follow democratic government could not have been stated before men knew that modern democratic government would follow aristocratic government in the West, and very few men were aware of this before 1800. Indeed, interest in the next stage of political development beyond democracy remained negligible until democratic government was firmly established in Northwestern Europe. Moreover, government by experts is government by social scientists, and the appearance of social science is almost as recent as the appearance of modern democratic government. Thus we need not go back in history very far to find the first faint adumbrations of the theory that democratic government in advanced nations will be followed by expert government, defined as government by social scientists chosen by such scientists.

It may be suggested that the ancient Greeks practiced political democracy, and also thought about the next stage in political evolution. It is true, of course, that Plato and Aristotle wrote about ideal states ruled by a philosopher king or by a moral elite, but both social conditions and scientific ideas were then so different from their modern equivalents that a review of their political proposals would scarcely be relevant here.

SAINT SIMON

Probably the first modern thinker to adumbrate the idea of government by experts was that brilliant but confused eccentric, the Comte de Saint Simon. He noted with satisfaction that the first Napoleon had surrounded himself with intellectuals and experts. He urged and predicted a great increase in the political power of such men. For instance, he proposed the creation of a parliament of intellectuals that would promote and control scientific research and public education. He admitted that he had been inspired by Condorcet's farsighted prediction that ultimately all enlightened peoples would advance their geniuses to the forefront of society. Condorcet himself had attributed this idea to Francis Bacon (*The New Atlantis*). But Saint Simon feared the rise of a permanent, professional bureaucracy. His ideal was a government dominated by businessmen advised by experts.[1]

THE CONSERVATIVE ELITISTS

Another strand of thought leading toward the idea of government by experts has been the conservative elitist criticism of political democracy.

The gradual rise and expansion of capitalist democracy was one of the most important social trends of the nineteenth century. Like all major long-run social trends it was beneficial, but, nevertheless, it had critics as well as advocates. Some supporters of the trend argued unwisely that democracy would benefit mankind because it would place political power in the hands of the great majority of common men or workers, who knew their own interests better and would advance them more effectively than any other class of rulers or voters. A few conservative thinkers tried to refute this argument by replying that every kind of past society had had, and every future one will have, a small ruling class that exploits the vast majority of men for its own benefit. They also argued that most voters in democratic states are incompetent and that therefore national leaders ought not to be compelled to seek their votes. We shall call these critics conservative elitists.

The first prominent conservative elitist was Gaetano Mosca (1848-1941), Professor of Political Science at the University of Milan and a member of the Italian Senate. He was the first to proclaim that every society—past, present, and future—must be controlled by a small ruling elite. He opposed the rise of democratic government. In his last important work, *The Ruling Class* (1939), revised in 1923, he asserted that democratic government had already enjoyed its best days and would soon disappear. The Italian Fascists honored him and thought they were making this prediction come true.

The most influential conservative elitist was the Italian engineer and economist, Vilfredo Pareto (1848-1923). He popularized the basic elitist doctrines and developed a detailed theory of the "circulation" or rise and fall of members of the elite. In *The Mind and Society* (1935) he predicted that the elites in all democratic countries would be repeatedly changed or replaced by revolution. Mussolini was an admirer of Pareto.

The conservative elitists did not suggest or predict a future transformation of democratic government into government by experts. Rather they stressed the claim that all governments are actually undemocratic because all are ruled by small elites. This does not imply that no change in the form of government is possible, but it does imply that such changes in form are unimportant. Thus the elitists not only failed to predict rule by an elite of experts, but implied that such a change would have no major consequences on political policies. My thesis is quite different. It asserts both that rule by political meritocrats is coming and that they will govern far better than any previous elite.

The theory that feudal states are ruled by a small elite is, of course, very old. And the theory that capitalist states are ruled by a small ruling class, the capitalists, was not new. It had been repeatedly stated by socialists before Mosca endorsed it. The major new element in conservative elitist doctrine was the claim that any new social order, even a socialist society, would necessarily be governed by a small, largely hereditary, ruling class that would exploit the rest of the nation.

Italy was a politically and economically backward part of Europe when Mosca and Pareto wrote. The real, but unstated reason why they attacked the theory of democratic government was that they believed such government would greatly reduce the political and economic advantages of the still half-feudal ruling elite in Italy. Indeed, they feared that it would lead to socialism, the ultimate evil in their opinion.

In 1943 James Burnham, an American philosopher and ex-Trotskyite, published *The Machiavellians, Defenders of Freedom*, which reviews and defends the elitist doctrines of Mosca, Pareto, and other conservative elitists. Burnham's principal thesis is that these men were more realistic and scientific than the optimistic advocates of democracy and socialism. This thesis has not been supported by the course of events since they wrote. Their dire predictions concerning the imminent failure of democracy and socialism have not been fulfilled. And the Nazis and Fascists who claimed to accept and apply their doctrines have been badly defeated.

After summarizing the principal common ideas of the earlier conservative elitists, Burnham goes on to apply them to three problems, one of which is, "Can Politics be Scientific?" In discussing this question he considers the possibility of government by "a scientific ruling group" (pp. 299-304).

He believes that scientific government would be beneficial, but adds that "there are obstacles in the way of scientific political action by an elite, which, if they are not quite insuperable . . . are nevertheless very formidable" (p. 303). First, it is very "difficult for men to be scientific, or logical, about social and political problems," especially when personal interests and privileges are affected. Second:

> A dilemma confronts any section of the elite that tries to act scientifically. The political life of the masses and the cohesion of society demand the acceptance of myths. A scientific

attitude towards society does not permit belief in the truth of the myths. But the leaders must profess, indeed foster, belief in the myths (p. 304).

It is hard for scientists to lie, and when they do so they often persuade and deceive themselves. For both reasons, "the possibility of scientific political rule depends upon favorable and temporary circumstances."

There is some merit in his first point, especially today, and he was speaking of current conditions. I shall explain later why I believe social scientists will become much more scientific and objective in the future.

His second point, concerning the need for social myths, is quite unconvincing. The fact that in the past men have accepted many myths does not prove that such acceptance was beneficial or that belief in myths will be beneficial in the future. It seems much more likely that the continued growth of social science and education will weaken belief in political, as well as religious, myths.

It is noteworthy that, although the conservative elitists attacked democracy and socialism, they did believe it possible to create, and did try to create, scientific social theories. They were not anti-intellectual or anti-scientific, as many conservative thinkers have been.

THE SOCIALIST ELITISTS

While the conservative elitists defended aristocratic-plutocratic political elites, a Polish socialist-syndicalist contemporary predicted with regret the rise of an intellectual-technical ruling elite. When living as a political prisoner in Siberia (1892-98), Waclaw Machajski (pronounced Vatzlov Makhayski) wrote a book[2] in which he predicted that the victory of the socialist parties would bring to power a new non-hereditary class of educated experts, intellectuals, and administrators. This class, he reasoned, is so small it can now have little political influence working alone. It cannot count on the support of, or alliance with, older ruling classes, and therefore must temporarily throw in its lot with the rising working classes, who badly need educated leaders and theorists. But, after the socialist movement has won political power, this educated elite will fill all higher government offices and run the government primarily for its own benefit.

In spite of this pessimistic theory, Machajski continued to advocate a blend of anarchism and socialism. He hoped that the power of the coming ruling class, the intellectual class, could be sufficiently curbed by limiting their incomes to the level of the average worker, and by expanding education until all workers belonged to the educated, ruling class. Those ends should be achieved by frequent strikes to enforce workers' demands.

When he returned to Russia after the 1917 revolution, he repeatedly restated these views, until forced into exile again. He argued that only equality of income could assure equality of educational opportunity. Yet the Soviet Union has since achieved a remarkable and unprecedented degree of equality of educational opportunity in a society with great differences in personal income. One must admit, nevertheless, that Machajski was much more prescient than any of his fellow elitists. He was probably the first to predict the rise of an intellectual-technical ruling elite.

In 1911 the German ex-socialist and ex-syndicalist Robert Michels published *Political Parties*,[3] in which he argued that political democracy is impossible because the masses are politically incompetent. He stated an "iron law of oligarchy, namely that human society will always be divided into those who lead and those who obey." This is essentially the theory of Mosca and Pareto, but Michels tried to verify it by a study of socialist political parties, and he was most interested in applying it to the coming socialist societies. He predicted that these would be ruled by socialist party bureaucrats, not by the working class, and he lamented this prospect.[4]

Machajski's views on the role of the intellectual class under socialism were publicized in America by Max Nomad in a series of books and articles, beginning with *Rebels and Renegades* (1932) and ending with *Aspects of Revolt*. Nomad accepted most of Machajski's thesis but he was more pessimistic. In *As-*

pects of Revolt he predicted that socialist states would not make personal incomes equal, and that inequality of income would preserve or recreate gross inequality of educational opportunity (chapter 2). Thus the new ruling class would be self-perpetuating.

Nomad thought that Machajski, Michels, himself, and others had largely anticipated James Burnham's theory of the managerial revolution. Their theory, he alleges, "became the subject of a best-selling book [*The Managerial Revolution*] by an author who gave no credit to his predecessors. He was a teacher of ethics" (p. 152).

There is some justification for this complaint. But Burnham was describing mainly the rise of professional business managers to the control of great private corporations, while Nomad and his forerunners were talking about the rise of an intellectual oligarchy in a socialist state. Moreover, Burnham did later write a book, *The Machiavellians*, in which he reviewed and gave full credit to some of his predecessors (but not to Machajski and Nomad).

Why do elitists believe that any new socialist society must be governed by a small ruling class? Their treatment of this point has been very brief and superficial. To state their case at all persuasively, one must read as much between as in their lines. The chief argument, often implicit rather than explicit, seems to be that the future will resemble the past. Because all previous societies have been governed by largely hereditary elites, all future societies will be so governed.

The unstated essential assumption here is that most or all of the conditions responsible for hereditary elite government in the past will continue in the future. These conditions include wide variations in individual health, personality, and intelligence, as well as social institutions that favor hereditary aristocracy or oligarchy. But such institutions can be changed or replaced. Private inheritance of power and property can be virtually eliminated, and all men can be given nearly equal educational and economic opportunities. Thus, the conclusion that all future democratic and/or socialist states will be ruled by hereditary elites is unjustified. On the other hand elitist doctrines have often suggested that rule by a natural elite is, or may become, desirable. In this respect, they anticipated the theory of government by experts.

It may be worthwhile here to stress the difference between rule by an hereditary political and/or economic elite—the traditional system—and rule by an hereditary natural elite. The latter would be based on inherited ability only, the former on inherited political office or wealth. The elitists who defend the traditional system usually try to obscure or minimize the difference between it and rule by an hereditary natural elite. It is true that hereditary political and economic elites have a higher average intelligence than the rest of the population, but these elites never include more than a very small minority of those persons with the highest inherited ability. Thus, the substitution of meritocracy, plutocracy, or capitalist democracy would replace over 80 percent of the existing elite with new and superior men. Moreover, the holdovers would have to study and work much harder to keep up with their new competitors and colleagues.

THE FABIANS

Another and stronger current of thought leading to the creation of a theory of government by experts is that which has for a hundred and fifty years increasingly advocated the use of such experts as political advisors. Shirley R. Letwin has plausibly contended that some recent participants in this doctrinal trend—notably Sidney and Beatrice Webb—have consciously or unconsciously rejected political democracy and advocated government by experts without admitting or recognizing that they have done so.[5] She begins by noting that John Stuart Mill had recommended the creation of a legislative commission, consisting of experts in government, which would not only assist Parliament in drafting new laws but, Letwin believes, would have also been authorized to draft proposed laws on its own initiative.[6]

Letwin asserts that the Webbs went much further, in their

A Review of Relevant Earlier Doctrines

Constitution for the Socialist Commonwealth of Great Britain (1920):

> They paraded the virtues of experts (attached to Parliamentary committees) but not their true function. . . . They advocated a form of government in which every effort would be made to win popular support for the acts of government [determined by experts] by making the people feel that they themselves had chosen the policies which had in fact been made by others. [However, they] did not acknowledge that their plan did away with democratic control, . . ."[7]

Whether or not the Webbs did in fact go as far as Letwin claims —I do not think they did—her claim illustrates one effect of their proposals. It also suggests a possible transition stage between political democracy and government by experts.

The Webbs clearly recognized and approved the growing role of experts as advisors to democratic legislators and administrators, but they did not suggest full government by experts, the assignment of final policy decisions to experts chosen by experts. Instead, in their constitution they asserted that "what is wrong with the world today is not too much Democracy but too little, not too many thoroughly democratic institutions but too few" (p. 89). They were eager to make democratic government more efficient and more extensive, not to replace it by expert government. However, they did recommend a great increase in the use of expert advisors by legislative bodies.

George Bernard Shaw, another pioneer Fabian, went further. In *Everybody's Political What's What* (1945) he advised that only experts in government should be allowed to become candidates for political office, because "the Everymans are so ignorant or miseducated economically, politically, scientifically, and religiously that they can neither govern themselves nor choose their governors wisely. . . . Rulers must be persons born with relevant special aptitudes and special abilities, and acquire an executive technique . . ." (p. 345). But Shaw was willing to allow expert rulers to be selected by all voters. He did not predict a new stage in political evolution. He thought of his proposal as one more reform in democratic government, and he apparently believed this reform is already feasible and desirable, or very soon will be. He was not writing about the distant future, as I am.

In *A Modern Utopia* (1905), H. G. Wells vaguely described an ideal government by an educated non-hereditary elite, the "Samurai." They would include nearly all educated, creative people—artists, poets, musicians, doctors, lawyers—as well as social scientists. Most of his discussion deals with rules of personal conduct—the Samurai cannot drink, smoke, or use drugs, and they are not allowed to act, sing, recite, or play games in public. They must be chaste and religious, and wear simple uniforms. They cannot engage in trade or lend money for interest. They are selected largely by educational and performance tests, but no detail concerning such tests or concerning the election of top national legislators and executives is given. However, Wells did revive and popularize Plato's ancient idea of government by a superior natural elite. And, unlike the conservative elitists, he was not opposing the rise of democratic government but anticipating a later stage of political evolution.

Wells's belief that artists, poets, musicians, and other creative persons who are not social scientists are especially fitted to rule a modern industrial society is irrational. It is difficult to understand how anyone as science-minded as Wells could have adopted it.

THE TECHNOCRATS

The first American movement to openly advocate both socialism and government by experts was Technocracy, long led by Howard Scott, which attracted considerable popular attention in the 1930's. The technocrats proposed that each industry be reorganized as a national monopoly. In *Life in a Technocracy* (1933), Harold Loeb, one of their chief early spokesmen, asserted that in technocracy "these corporate monopolies would be the government" (p. 78). He suggested that the boards of directors of these monopolies should consist of retired chief executives and research scientists, and that these boards should "choose

A Review of Relevant Earlier Doctrines

their ablest members to represent them on the coordinating industrial board," the national government. Its chairman would be the chief executive. He called this "a most undemocratic system" (p. 79). All officials of the corporate monopolies were to be appointed from above; and monopoly directors, by the chief executive of the national government. These men were to be engineers not business executives or public administrators.

"Administration, in a technocracy, has to do with material factors which are subject to measurement," Loeb reasoned:

> Therefore, popular voting can be largely dispensed with. It is stupid deciding an issue by vote or opinion when a yardstick can be used. . . . Voting on . . . questions for which there is a right answer and a wrong answer would be even more farcical than voting for President. To trained minds in possession of complete information, the answer in nearly every case would be incontrovertible (p. 75).

These claims were premature in 1933, but they will become more and more persuasive as the decades pass.

The outstanding feature, and the great fallacy, of technocratic theory was the doctrine that all economic and other social problems can and should be solved by engineers, not by social scientists. Reacting to the fact that most social scientists had always studied and defended the existing social system, the technocrats concluded that they were incompetent to deal with the problems of a new social system. The technocrats were unaware that many basic principles of social science are applicable to any social system. They failed to appreciate the obvious benefits of specialization in science. They naively believed that men trained in chemical, electrical, or mechanical engineering could treat social problems more expertly than men trained in the social sciences.

THE MANAGERIALISTS

Another, quite separate, line of thought suggesting the rise of government by experts goes back to a brilliant and very influential book, *The Modern Corporation and Private Property* (1932), by A. A. Berle, Jr., and G. C. Means. They were the first to popularize the vital conclusion that the growth of large corporations gradually creates a non-owning managerial class free from control by stockholders. These managers are themselves becoming more professional in education and point of view. In time, such highly educated professional managers will control nearly all large corporations, which will perform most economic activities.

In his stimulating and controversial work, *The Managerial Revolution* (1941), James Burnham carried this line of thought much further and boldly predicted the rapid rise of a managerial society, a socialist society ruled by managers of production, the kind of men Berle and Means had written about. He attributed this coming revolution to the defects of capitalism rather than to the defects of democratic government. In the coming managerial society "the state . . . will own and control the instruments of production" (p. 72), and the state itself will be controlled undemocratically by the managers, who will constitute a new ruling class. This new society will not be a socialist society because there will be a ruling class (p. 120), but it may well be *"called"* socialist (his italics, p. 122).

According to James Burnham, all advanced countries are in the process of evolution from capitalism to a managerial society, but in 1940 the U.S.S.R., Nazi Germany, and Fascist Italy had come closest to achieving it (p. 152). And among these three the U.S.S.R. has approached it most closely:

> But structurally at any rate, the institutions of present-day Russia, more fully than any others in the world, give the direction toward the future. It is along such lines that the institutions of established and consolidated managerial society will evolve (p. 221).

The Managerial Revolution includes a chapter each on the Russian way and the German way to the managerial society. He predicted that the American way would be closer to the Nazi German way than to the Soviet way (p. 270). It might proceed "in a comparatively democratic fashion" but would more likely involve "revolutionary mass movements, terror, purges," and other undemocratic processes (p. 272).

He thought that "the 1940 presidential election . . . may well have been the last regular presidential election in the history of this country" (p. 261), and he predicted that the transition to a managerial society in America and the world would be largely completed by 1970, some fifty years after its beginning (p. 71).

Although he anticipated that the managerial revolution would be violent and would require a period of undemocratic government, he predicted that "with the consolidation of the structure of managerial society, its dictatorial phase (totalitarianism) will change into a democratic phase" (p. 167). However, for him democratic government is always a form of rule by a small ruling class (p. 163), which in this case would be the managers of production. Once in power, the managers would find it easy to control democratic elections: "The control of the state by the managers will be suitably guaranteed by appropriate political institutions, analogous to the guarantee of bourgeois dominance under capitalism by the bourgeois political institutions" (p. 72). No further detail on the structure and methods of government by managers is given.

There is hardly any discussion of the defects of democratic government in this book. As noted earlier, Burnham shared the anti-democratic views of the conservative elitists, but for him the managerial revolution was inevitable because of the defects of capitalism, not because of the faults of democratic government. Like Marx and Engels, he charged that capitalism had inherent defects which make its replacement by a new politico-economic system inevitable. His indictment includes several old socialist charges (chapter 3), such as the dubious claim that a capitalist society cannot eliminate mass unemployment (p. 31), and a new or rare charge that capitalist states cannot wage war efficiently because war is unprofitable (p. 267).

Burnham used the term "managers" to designate those who manage the process of production in private industry or government. He excluded the senior corporate executives and financiers concerned primarily with "guiding the company towards a profit" (p. 83). Apparently, like Veblen, he regarded them as unproductive or counterproductive. But he criticized Veblen for assuming that engineers do or should manage production.

Burnham explicitly included many senior government bureaucrats in the managerial class. He discussed at some length the question of whether his managerial society should instead be called a bureaucratic society (pp. 155-60), and concluded that this is a trivial, verbal question. In the managerial socialist society, nearly all managers would be bureaucrats, and they would perform functions previously performed by both private and public managers.

Perhaps the most distinctive—for our purpose—characteristic of Burnham's managers is that they were men trained and experienced in the management of production, not in the solution of social problems. They were all managers or administrators, not social scientists or social engineers. He had nothing to say about legislators or a national legislature.

Perhaps because he was a philosopher, not a social scientist, Professor Burnham failed to understand the radical difference between the skills and functions of social scientists and those of managers of production. The former are trained and experienced in the solution of social problems, like reducing unemployment; the latter in the administration of public and private enterprises. Thus his claim that managers have a distinctive operational bias towards "solving social and political problems" (p. 92) is as unsound as the Technocratic claim that engineers are peculiarly fitted to solve political and economic problems. Like the Technocrats, Burnham ignored the vital fact that social scientists alone are properly trained to solve social problems. The chief difference between my thesis and his is that I emphasize this fact and therefore predict rule by social scientists, whereas he ignored it and predicted political rule by managers of production.

To sum up, Burnham's *The Managerial Revolution* is one of the four or five earlier books that came closest to stating the thesis of this one, but there are radical differences. Burnham predicted the rapid rise of managerial socialism. He failed to distinguish between the rise of socialism and the rise of government by managers, and he expected that, after managerial socialism had become firmly established, it would restore democratic government. He talked much about the evils of capitalism and little about the evils of democracy. In this book I feature the latter, and predict the rise of undemocratic government by experts after socialism has been firmly established. However, I do not regard socialism as a prerequisite for government by experts, which I consider inevitable whether or not socialism is adopted.

SANTAYANA AND JORDAN

The eminent philosopher George Santayana was born in Spain, an undemocratic country, and never learned to appreciate political democracy. He not only defended monarchy, aristocracy, and Mussolini—he chose to live out the last years of his life in Fascist Italy—but, in *Reason and Society* (1905), also proposed a new ideal form of undemocratic government:

> This would be timocracy—a government by men of merit. . . . Such a timocracy (of which the Roman Church is a good example) would differ from the social aristocracy that now exists only by the removal of hereditary advantages. People would be born equal, but they would grow unequal, and the only equality subsisting would be equality of opportunity . . . a full development of timocracy would allow the proved leader to gain great ascendancy (pp. 128-29).

Santayana did not explain more precisely how ideal rulers should be chosen. The above quotation vaguely suggests success in one's occupation as a basis, and co-option as a method, of selection. No consideration is given to professional training and experience in government or social science. Like Plato, Santayana may have thought eminent philosophers could be ideal rulers.

His chief argument for government by the most able men was simply that men differ widely in ability and that the most able men can govern much better than the average man or his elected representative. He recognized that hereditary aristocrats were often incompetent, and therefore advocated rule by natural aristocrats. He indicted democracy for ignoring natural inequality: "We count heads as if we paid out money by weight, without asking whether it was gold or silver."[8]

Santayana's entire discussion of his proposed timocracy fills less than two pages. Obviously he had devoted little thought to it and made little effort to secure serious consideration of it.

Another much less well-known conservative American philosopher, Elijah Jordan, a contemporary of Santayana's, proposed a similar system of government. In his *Theory of Legislation* (1930), he advocated government by an intellectual elite, "a corporate class of free intellects whose speculative imagination is allowed to wander at will . . . ; and whose hand is . . . absolutely unhindered in the process of experimental verification. . . ."[9] These experts would be organized in a system of cultural institutions. The institutions, not the individual men, should directly control the state.

Jordan was vague as to how the members of this elite would be selected. He apparently relied on "the judgment that wills the unity of the social order," which is located in "the judiciary."[10] This is not a very logical or practical proposal, and Jordan did not predict its adoption.

Neither Santayana nor Jordan seem to have recognized that social scientists know more about social and political problems than poets and philosophers. Apparently they wanted the ruling elite to include the most able men in every occupation.

MICHAEL YOUNG

The most comprehensive, readable, and stimulating recent discussion of government by experts is to be found in a curious book which—imitating Bellamy's *Looking Backward*—purports to be a review of English history from 1870 to 2033, written in the latter year. *The Rise of Meritocracy, 1870-2033*, by the English Fabian socialist Michael Young, describes, predicts, and

A Review of Relevant Earlier Doctrines

explains the rise of meritocracy during these years. Because the author's account is somewhat ironic, it is difficult to tell when to take him seriously. If he believes that any country will be almost completely meritocratic by 2033, he is unrealistic and visionary. On the other hand, by condensing this trend into a short period of time, he may perhaps be able to arouse greater public interest in it.

Writing purportedly in 2033, he describes English meritocracy as follows:

> Today we frankly recognize that democracy can be no more than aspiration, and have rule not so much by the people as by the cleverest people; not an aristocracy of birth, not a plutocracy of wealth, but a true meritocracy of talent. . . . Today each member of the meritocracy has an attested minimum [I.Q.?] rating of 125 (with the top posts for psychologists, sociologists and Permanent Secretaries reserved . . . for the over 160's) . . . (pp. 18-20).

His reference to "psychologists" and "sociologists" suggests that for him political meritocracy means government by experts in social science. He also makes clear that meritocracy requires achievement of equality of opportunity in education.

He attributes the growth of meritocracy primarily to the rise of Fabian socialism, the Labour Party in particular, and to the resulting growth and democratization of public education. However, he condemns the Labour Party campaign for a single-channel, American-style school system and predicts that the ruling elite of the future will from an early age be segregated in superior schools or school channels.

Most of his discussion deals with the rise of meritocracy in general, not with that of political meritocracy, but of course the same causes or reasons are responsible for both trends. In a section on the "Decline of Parliament," he notes the chief defect of democracy: "The mother of a problem family in Brighouse . . . had the same vote as a Beatrice Webb" (p. 107). And he stresses the growing complexity of political problems.

Young does not predict the elimination, but merely the radical reform of parliament. The House of Commons will become a grievance committee democratically chosen but with the power of complaint only. The House of Lords will be filled with the most eminent and able men in the nation and will rule the country, as the Commons now does. Its members will be selected, not elected, but Young does not explain the method of selection. His discussion of the decline of parliament is only four pages long. It is based on Bernard Shaw's theories.

Unfortunately, Young's credibility as a scientific forecaster of social trends is reduced by some obviously absurd predictions. For instance, he predicts that in a single typical future peacetime year (2031) the British national real income will rise by 54 percent, but real wage rates will remain unchanged (p. 128). He also anticipates that by 2031 wages will be equal for all workers (pp. 126-27). Other such extravagant predictions could be cited.

The final chapter of *The Rise of Meritocracy*, the longest in this little (160-page) book, is devoted to an explanation of a "Crisis" resulting from popular dissatisfaction with meritocracy in 2033. This is far less clear and plausible than any of the earlier chapters, but it suggests that the auth r does not personally favor the rise of meritocracy, or at least that he is very dubious as to its merits. His arguments against meritocracy will be reviewed in chapter 6.

H. W. ELDREDGE

The most significant recent American book suggesting the rise of government by experts in government is *The Second American Revolution, the Near Collapse of Traditional Democracy* (1964) by H. Wentworth Eldredge, an American sociologist.

In the opening sentence of his first chapter, Eldredge asserts that

> Western democracy is impaled on the sharp horns of a dilemma; unless a highly motivated, intelligent, and ethical elite can be discovered, trained, and given powerful tools . . . to plan, direct, and control, our society may be defeated by the Communist bloc in the struggle to direct the future of man-

A Review of Relevant Earlier Doctrines

kind. If, however, such an aristocracy of talent does dominate, will Western society remain democratic and free? (p. 1)

Eldredge advocates the second alternative. He does not explain how the elite rulers should be chosen, but he does claim that

> ... modern society is too valuable to be entrusted to a mechanical majority of the citizens, ill-equipped by ability, training, inclination and time to grapple with problems of a civilization and world that probably no one does understand too well (pp. 284-85).

Most of his book is devoted to a discussion of past elites, Communism, social classes, Fascism, the managerial revolution, American education, and proposed reforms in American political structure (such as centralization and strengthening of the executive). Indeed, his thesis concerning government by experts is largely buried in his treatment of these other subjects. It is stated much more clearly, completely, and compactly in a sarcastic review by James Real in the *Saturday Review* for June 6, 1964. Real is so conventional in his thinking that he assumes that a mere summary of Eldredge's thesis is enough to refute it. Like most men, he apparently thinks that if a social theory is novel and radical, it is necessarily absurd and deserves no serious consideration.

My chief criticism of Eldredge is that he did not state his thesis as clearly, completely, and often as he should have. Indeed, it is a mere adumbration of a theory. Moreover, I think his stress on alleged current crisis is unjustified. Social change is inevitably slow and gradual. In advanced states, governments are now more efficient than ever before, and they will certainly become increasingly efficient. It is this gradual, long-continuing trend, not a current crisis, which will eventually bring about the achievement of government by experts. Nevertheless, the number of American social scientists who have even briefly advocated or predicted the rise of government by experts chosen by experts is still so very small that Eldredge's proposal may be influential.

His book contains a long review of the history of political

doctrine, but this review covers none of the forerunners discussed in this chapter. It is devoted primarily to men who wrote before 1800, and to other ideas than government by experts.

GENERAL NEGLECT OF THE IDEA OF GOVERNMENT BY EXPERTS

Some concluding remarks on the contributors to the theory of government by experts are now appropriate. This review of doctrine is not meant to be complete, but it is far more complete than any previously published, and it covers men who did no more than faintly adumbrate a part of the basic idea of government by experts.

None of the writers discussed above clearly and explicitly advocated or predicted the replacement of democratic government by expert government, defined as rule by social scientists chosen by social scientists. Young and Eldredge came closer to doing so than anyone else. But Young wrote a fictional account—like Orwell's *1984*—apparently intended to warn men of a serious threat, not to advocate or predict a coming inevitable social change. And Eldredge merely urged, in very general terms, a much more complete reliance on experts in government. He did not suggest a specific form of expert government. And he did not predict the rise of government by experts.

Perhaps the most surprising fact revealed by the above review of the scant literature on, or hinting at, government by experts is the lack of discussion of this idea by political scientists. My review covers the contributions of one famous dramatist (Shaw), three philosophers (Santayana, Jordan, and Burnham), four economists (Pareto, J. S. Mill, the Webbs, and Young), two sociologists (Saint Simon and Eldredge), two socialist theoreticians (Michels and Machajski), but only one political scientist (Mosca), an Italian who did his major work before 1900 and certainly did not discuss government by experts. So far as I am aware, no political scientist has ever stated or discussed the idea of government by experts, as here defined.

As further evidence of past neglect of the theory of government by experts, and of the as yet negligible influence of the above writers on political scientists, I wish to cite some very recent books on democratic government. *The Problem of Democracy* (revised edition, 1965) by Herbert Tingsten is an acute study of the history and theory of democratic government. The last two chapters are devoted to dictatorship, the chief competitor of democracy. The idea that democratic government might be replaced by expert government is completely ignored.

The same criticism applies to *Democracy and Elitism, Two Essays with Selected Readings* (1967) by Harry K. Girvetz, an able liberal political scientist. As the title indicates, about half of this book is devoted to an essay and nine readings on elitism, and expert government is a form of elitism, but Girvetz does not mention government by experts. His readings are taken largely from authors who defended aristocracy against the rise of democracy. He offers no comments on or readings from authors who both approve of the rise of democracy and look forward to a new post-democratic form of elitism, political meritocracy.

Again, one would surely expect that a book entitled *The Myth of the Ruling Class* would contain at least a brief reference to the modern theory that every advanced state will in time be ruled by an elite of experts in government. But in fact James H. Meisel published in 1956 a 432-page book with this title that does not even briefly mention this theory. It is true that he deliberately set out to state and criticize Mosca's doctrine of elite government, but how can a critic evaluate one doctrine of elite government without comparing it with competing theories of elite government? Meisel apparently failed to make such a comparison because he had never heard of the new and rarely stated doctrine set forth in this book. He defines "elitism" as "at its crudest the notion that the Few should rule because they do in fact rule, and less crudely the contention that, since only a few can rule, the Many do not and never will" (p. 3). This definition does not include the theory of government by experts, obviously a variety of elitism.

Finally, it is noteworthy that a 1964 collection of essays

edited by W. J. Stankiewitz, *Political Thought Since World War II*—a title that suggests comprehensive coverage of major new ideas—contains no discussion of political meritocracy or government by experts. Indeed, the terms "meritocracy," "experts," and "elite" are not listed in the nine-page index. And because thirty-one different authors contributed to this book, it reflects a general attitude among leading political scientists.[11]

In sum, my review of some thirty hints at or adumbrations of the theory of government by experts should not lead the reader to conclude that the thesis of this book has been widely discussed or that it has been seriously defended by any influential political scientist.

THE REASONS FOR THE NEGLECT

Why have political scientists and other writers ignored or neglected the idea of government by experts chosen by experts? Some of the reasons will be suggested later when I discuss the principal arguments against this proposal, but stated arguments rarely reveal all of the real reasons for opposition to a new idea and this is especially true of the arguments against government by experts. In any case, a tentative summary of such undeclared reasons seems appropriate here.

I suggest first of all that some social scientists still believe that the political system of their nation is divinely ordained, and that those who propose or predict a radical change in it are at least slightly impious or wicked. This point of view has been declining for centuries, but still affects many educated men, unconsciously if not consciously, even in advanced countries. That is one reason why Fascists and Communists are often called wicked men.

Another closely related and more influential reason is that in democratic countries many intellectuals who have wholly or largely abandoned religion believe that democratic government is the one and only moral, fair, or just form of government. In other words, they believe strongly that those who propose to change this form of government are making an immoral or unethical proposal. For them, democracy is not merely expedient or utilitarian, but moral and ethical. And all moral theory has absolute and enduring validity. What is immoral today cannot become moral tomorrow, or even a century or two later. That is why so many moralists oppose changes in the laws on divorce, birth control, abortion, obscenity, homosexual behavior, and so forth. Their attitude towards the abolition of democracy is based on the same logic. Thus, they often call those who oppose political democracy immoral.

A third and still more important reason is that many men believe they benefit from the existing political system and are therefore reluctant to discuss any radical change in it, or to support financially anyone who proposes such a change. In general, those who have acquired wealth, power, and/or prestige in democratic countries are inclined to attribute their success in part to the existing political system. They fear that any radical change in this system would endanger their continual success, or that of their children.

The fourth reason is that men motivated by the religious, philosophic, or conservative motives noted above have very great influence on publishers, broadcasting stations, universities, and governments. They are in a strong position to prevent original thinkers from publishing, broadcasting, or teaching unpopular new ideas such as that of government by experts. In democratic countries, of course, such censorship is rarely overt, but it is nevertheless surprisingly effective. Every writer on social science must censor his own writings in order to get them published and read. Every professor of social science must censor his lectures so that they will not offend the parents of his students or his own colleagues and academic superiors.

On the other hand, such conservative opposition to an even more serious threat to vested interests, namely the threat of socialism, has been unable to prevent a long-continuing, detailed discussion of socialist ideas. Thus there must be other, special reasons for the nearly complete neglect of the idea of government by experts.

The most important such special reason may be that there

is no new rising social class that would benefit from the rise of government by experts. The introduction of democratic government was strongly supported by the rising middle class, who felt hindered, humbled and exploited by the nobility. The rise of socialism has been vigorously and patiently supported by another rising social class, the proletariat. But there is no such powerful new class to advocate the adoption of government by experts. I shall argue later that the growth of the intellectual and professional classes will increase support for government by experts, but government by experts will not be government by or for these classes. It will be government by social scientists, who will constitute less than 5 percent of all professionals, and less than 1 percent of the population. And they will rule for the benefit of society as a whole, not for the benefit of the intellectual and professional classes.

Another important special reason for the relative neglect of the idea of government by social scientists is that social science is very new and most of its theories are still controversial. Moreover, social scientists are by training much more sceptical and cautious than the pioneer socialist thinkers, who were convinced that they had discovered a certain cure for most of the evils of their age. Social scientists fully realize that their science is in a very early stage of development, and those few who have thought of government by experts may have believed it premature to predict a radical change for which the scientific evidence is still very incomplete.

Finally, many social scientists believe that the function of social science is description and explanation of past and present social systems, not the reform, let alone the radical transformation, of their own social system. For instance, the so-called new welfare economists deny that economists can determine whether any proposed social reform would increase welfare. They assign all, or nearly all, such judgments to moralists or moralistic voters. And many other social scientists assert that, as scientists, they can describe what is, but cannot determine what ought to be.

In this book, of course, I am predicting what will be, not

A Review of Relevant Earlier Doctrines

prescribing what ought to be, but I also argue that we can predict what will be, in part, by determining what ought to be, i.e., what will increase social welfare.

Although many social scientists deny that scientists can determine what ought to be, even in order to maximize nonmoral welfare, some are, paradoxically, more interested in what ought to be, for moral or religious reasons, than in what is or will be. Indeed, the same writers who claim that men cannot learn how to increase social or economic welfare often claim that they already know how to increase moral welfare or to evaluate social policies by moral standards.

3
Why Government by Experts Is Coming

INTRODUCTION

Let us turn now from the history of my thesis to the reasons why the rise of government by experts in government, political meritocracy, is inevitable.

The most general and basic reason is simply that this development is, or will become socially desirable, in other words that government by experts would be much more efficient in maximizing human welfare than any democratic government could be. In the long run, men always adopt major beneficial social reforms. Men often act unwisely, but they tend to act more and more rationally as the centuries pass. Moreover, the growth of science, education, and social reform is far more rapid today than ever before, and will speed up the coming rationalization of all social institutions.

Of course, this general and basic argument is not self-evident. It requires detailed support, and this chapter will be devoted to more specific arguments supporting it.

It is possible—indeed I think probable—that mankind will not grow wiser fast enough to prevent a catastrophic thermonculear war, or a series of such wars, which could delay the achievement of government by experts. It is difficult to estimate how long this delay might be, and I shall not attempt to do so here. However, I believe that mankind will survive and continue to progress along much the same lines as before, and that one of these lines will lead to the achievement of government by experts.

The performance of democratic governments can and will be improved in many ways. The need for such improvements is not a valid argument for government by experts. A change to government by experts can be justified only by very significant benefits that could not be achieved by the reform of democratic government.

Socialists have often argued that the adoption of socialism would make government far more democratic and efficient by eliminating the capitalists who now finance political campaigns, control newspapers and television stations, and often bribe legislators and government officials. I assume here that their argument is sound and that therefore government by experts is not inevitable because it is needed to eliminate these evils. Rather, I predict that socialism will be largely achieved and will virtually eliminate these evils in democratic countries before their citizens decide to replace democracy with government by experts.

The claim that the functions of government should or will eventually be entrusted to social scientists is based on the often unstated assumption that social problems can be solved, or rationally studied, only by scientific methods. This assumption is rejected by all religious and philosophic persons. Religious men believe that social as well as personal conduct should be guided, or at least influenced, by religious revelations. Philosophers believe that social conduct should be influenced, if not guided, by ethical principles that cannot be verified by scientific observation or experimentation.

Thus, to justify fully my prediction that the functions of government will eventually be entrusted to social scientists, I ought to explain why the methods used by scientists to solve social problems are superior to those used by theologians and philosophers. However, this thesis has been repeatedly stated and elaborated by social scientists and logical positivists. I have myself defended it in another book, *Religion, Philosophy, and Science*. I wish to devote this book to ideas not previously or adequately discussed elsewhere. Consequently, I shall assume here that social problems can be solved only by the application of scientific methods and that theologians and philosophers can contribute nothing to their solution, except when they anticipate, endorse, or duplicate the work of social scientists.

Let us turn now to more specific reasons why the rise of government by experts in government is inevitable. The first, and one of the most significant, is that most voters are, and will always remain, relatively incompetent to vote wisely.

VOTERS ARE INCOMPETENT

Even in advanced countries where semi-democracy has functioned longest and most successfully, the vast majority of voters are obviously incompetent. They do not have the education, experience, or interest required to evaluate proposed social policies or political candidates. The average American voter, the best educated in the world, still has less than a high school education, and few American high schools even try to give their graduates a good foundation in social science. Moreover, a career as a grocery store clerk, factory worker, civil engineer, etc., does not prepare one to evaluate proposed laws and foreign policies.

In his book, *The Public Philosophy* (1955), Walter Lippmann wrote:

> There is no mystery about why there is such a tendency for popular opinion to be wrong in judging war and peace. Strategic and diplomatic decisions call for a kind of knowledge—not to speak of an experience and a seasoned judgment—which cannot be had by glancing at newspapers, listening to snatches of radio comment, watching politicians perform on television, hearing occasional lectures, and reading a few books. It would not be enough to make a man competent to decide whether to amputate a leg, and it is not enough to qualify him to choose war or peace, to arm or not to arm, to intervene or to withdraw, to fight on or to negotiate (pp. 24-25).

Although Lippmann's words are specifically directed to problems of foreign policy, they apply with equal force to problems of domestic policy in democratic countries. The typical voter is so busy earning a living and raising a family that he has little time for or interest in the serious study of social problems and national policies.

To the average voter in a democratic state, social problems seem far less real and important than his personal problems. The great political questions of the day rank with him as minor leisure-hour interests, usually much less important than his sports and hobbies. And even among those seriously interested in politics leisure-hour attention is often arbitrarily restricted. It is widely considered in poor taste to discuss either politics or religion in social gatherings.

The individual voter is well aware that his vote is only one among many millions. Because his political influence is usually negligible, he does not consider it reasonable to make much effort to vote wisely. Even if he were eager to make this effort, he would find it difficult, if not impossible.

In the daily routine of a man's family or vocational life, he faces the same problems again and again, and learns from experience that certain decisions yield better results than others. He is also under the influence of relatively clear and simple personal motives and interests. But when he has to vote on social issues, or for political representatives, he faces unfamiliar problems, about which his personal experience tells him very little. And many complex and conflicting motives and interests are involved. Thus, he relies primarily on advice from men he believes to be more competent, but who, even if more competent, usually give advice designed to serve their own special interests, or those of their employers. Few voters are able to distinguish between experts and quacks, or between sound advice and propaganda.

These general conclusions about the incompetence of the average voter have been repeatedly verified by field studies. For instance, in 1948 public opinion surveys revealed that 10 percent of United States voters did not even know who was running for president. Much more significant is the finding in this year that 66 percent of the voters "had no knowledge of party platforms nor the foggiest idea where Truman and Dewey stood on the major issues of the campaign."

Similarly in 1958 an opinion survey revealed that barely half of the voters could name any of the Congressional candidates seeking their votes. In 1960, when American voters were asked what issues concerned them most, 32 percent could not name a single issue. In 1948, a survey found that only 33 percent of American voters could explain the main function of the United States State Department. An earlier survey had disclosed that 53 percent of voters had never heard of the United States Foreign Service.[1]

Most voters join the party their parents belonged to and vote the way their party leaders and newspapers tell them to. They are mere pawns in the hands of special interests.

I have been describing literate voters in prosperous countries with stable democratic governments. The situation is far worse in backward countries, yet most democratic theorists have failed to recognize this fact and its implications.

Modern Americans have been so well indoctrinated with the case for political democracy that the great majority of them actually believe that the illiterate and impoverished masses of China, India, Korea, and Vietnam are competent to select their rulers democratically. Indeed, it is the deliberate policy of the State Department to establish, or help to establish, democratic governments everywhere, and Communists are constantly and harshly criticized for establishing or maintaining undemocratic regimes in backward countries. But the illiterate, impoverished voters of undeveloped countries are incapable of making political democracy work. No backward country has ever been democratic for long. In India, the most plausible exception to this generalization, the ruling Congress Party has never been defeated, and recurrent defeat of the government is a criterion of democracy. The nominal democracy now prevailing in India will probably be replaced by a military or Communist dictatorship within a decade or two after the Congress Party is first defeated in national elections, if not before.

If the average voter is incompetent to determine the best social policies or select able rulers, the reader may ask why democratic governments have performed so well in advanced

Why Government by Experts Is Coming

countries like England and America. There are several reasons. First, the agencies that form public opinion in these countries are still controlled by a small oligarchy, men of education, wealth, and high social status. Moreover, this same small, well-educated class provides nearly all of the campaign funds necessary to win elections. Thus, the policies and personnel of democratic governments are largely determined, directly or indirectly, by a small elite of superior intelligence and education. Finally, these governments have had to compete only with less competent aristocratic or dictatorial governments.

In his *Patterns of Anti-Democratic Thought* (1949), perhaps the best recent summary of such thought, David Spitz, an ardent democrat, tries to refute the argument that the average voter is incompetent, or much less competent than the expert in government. He begins by stating the argument in a form that opens it to easy criticism, namely as the very general claim that the average man is unfit to govern. He then points out correctly that it is not the average man, but his representatives, who rule in a democratic state (p. 110). He thinks this is a crushing refutation. He seems unaware that the anti-democratic argument implies, and often explicitly states, that the average man is far less competent to select representatives to govern the country. This is my argument.

Spitz also attempts to prove that the average man is competent to elect good rulers by claiming that democratic governments have in fact governed more wisely than contemporary undemocratic governments (pp. 118-25). This claim is true, but, as noted above, it may be explained by the fact that so-called democracies are only semi-democratic; they are perhaps more plutocratic than democratic. Moreover, even if democracy works better than monarchy, aristocracy, or dictatorship, this does not prove that it will in the future function better than government by experts. And my basic thesis is not that democracy is inferior to previous forms of government, but that it is, or will become, much inferior to government, by experts in government.

To strengthen further his attempted refutation of the claim that the average man is unfit to govern, Spitz asserts that there is no such thing as an average man. This, of course, is a pure quibble. To answer it, one need only define "average man" as a man within a certain very broad class of men.

It may be suggested that, although the average voter of our time is incompetent to vote wisely, the continued progress of education and future eugenic measures will produce a capable electorate. I would reply that, as men become wiser, social problems will become ever more complex. Moreover, experts will improve their knowledge and skill faster than the average voter. A division of labor will therefore always be beneficial.

EXPERTS ARE COMPETENT

Government by experts would be more efficient than government by voters and democratically elected politicians because experts are more talented, better educated, more specialized, and more experienced than other voters and politicians. All experts should have advanced university degrees. Indeed, all experts in top jobs should have a Ph.D. or the equivalent. Because universities admit only superior persons, and graduate only the best of these, all experts are talented. Moreover, if experts in top jobs were chosen by their colleagues, only the more talented of them would be chosen.

Men vary enormously in their demonstrated abilities. The average man is far superior to feeble-minded men, and geniuses are far superior to average men. Indeed, there are very great differences even within small groups of very superior persons.

The wider the range of intelligence and ability among men, the greater is the superiority of the most talented, the stronger is the case for entrusting government leadership to a very gifted and able minority of experts in government. Because of the recent rapid growth of co-educational higher education, which throws superior young men and women together during the most marriageable ages, the proportion of marriages between very superior men and women is rising steadily in all advanced countries. Such marriages produce both many more gifted children and more highly gifted children than other marriages.

Why Government by Experts Is Coming

They widen the range of human ability and therefore make government by experts more desirable. When the children of these very superior children are in their turn segregated in the best universities—such as Harvard, Yale, or Stanford—they will also often marry each other and produce even more and superior geniuses. This trend will continue for centuries.

Even if men were equal in natural ability, an expert with a degree from West Point, plus several years of graduate studies and thirty years of military experience would make a far better general than an average man. Thus, generals should be experts. The same logic applies to legislators, judges, and public administrators.

Men who are elected and reelected to public office are, or gradually become, expert at winning elections—getting publicity, raising campaign funds, public speaking, etc. They rarely are, or become, expert at solving problems of legislation and public administration. It is true, of course, that a legislator reelected many times gradually learns more and more about legislation. It is equally true that a layman who practiced medicine for twenty years would gradually learn more and more about medicine. But it would be far better to have both legislators and doctors professionally trained before they begin to practice their professions.

A few professionally trained social scientists have been elected and reelected to public office. They are, or become, experts both at winning elections and at legislating or administering. But experts disagree with laymen on many social issues. Thus, if experts elected to public office fully apply their professional training, they vote or act in ways that alienate most voters. They therefore, either fail to be reelected or they learn to act as their supporters wish. *Democracy results in inexpert government even when experts are elected to office.*

One of the most obvious and important social trends of our time is the trend toward increasing specialization or division of labor. Every increase in the total body of knowledge makes specialization more necessary, and the volume of knowledge is expanding faster today than ever before. Furthermore, every increase in the scale of social and economic organization makes a greater division of labor economical, whether or not there has been an increase in knowledge. The substitution of government by experts for democratic government will be one of many steps toward greater specialization. It will substitute more specialized, and therefore more competent, legislators and chief executives for unspecialized or less specialized men.

Another reason why experts in government are more competent in government than voters and their elected representatives is that experts are relatively free from personal, occupational, and regional bias. Voters who work for chain stores usually vote against discriminatory taxes on such stores, while owners of small independent stores usually vote for such taxes. Men who work for steel mills usually vote for tariffs on steel imports. We could list thousands of such parochial factors. Most voters and politicians are strongly influenced by one or more of them. But experts working for or running a central government are much less influenced by such considerations.

If the top experts of a government run by experts were selected by their professional colleagues, they would be even more resistant than they now are to political pressure exercised by special-interest groups such as trade unions, trade associations, and regional political conditions. Such experts would not have to raise political campaign funds or please voters with parochial interests. They would only have to win and retain the support of highly educated, broad-minded fellow experts.

All social scientists have received some training in science and scientific method, and all training in scientific reasoning teaches men to be as objective and impartial as possible. It is more difficult to achieve such scientific thinking in the social sciences than in natural sciences, but prolonged exposure to scientific analysis and ideals must inevitably make social scientists much more objective and impartial than untrained voters and politicians.

A further reason why experts will be more competent rulers than politicians is that highly educated experts will be more eager to conduct numerous well-planned large-scale scientific

Why Government by Experts Is Coming

social experiments. Scientific experimentation is as essential for the development of social science as it is for the development of physics and chemistry. But voters and politicians untrained in any science are far less eager to promote social experiments than physical and chemical experiments, and they have too little interest in the latter.

A government run by social scientists might build several completely new cities, each of a radically different design, in order to observe scientifically the varying effects of life in different kinds of cities. It could and should conduct various experimental eugenics programs in different areas. It could test alternative weekly work schedules in different plants. It could experiment with proposed new educational methods in different school systems. America now has many school systems using varying methods, but the methods are rarely planned to test specific hypotheses, and the results are rarely observed and recorded by scientists.

I have been arguing that experts in government could govern more efficiently than non-experts. I now wish to argue a related but different point, namely that experts can evaluate and select fellow experts far more competently than laymen can do so.

To evaluate properly the performance of any expert, one must be an expert. The layman does not know what can be done or how it should be done. Only a person with similar professional training and experience can grade the work of an expert. The layman may be able to determine whether the results of some professional services are directly beneficial to him, but he cannot tell whether the results should have been still better, or the cost much less. Professional legislators and administrators should therefore be chosen by fellow professionals, not by laymen.

In *The New Belief in the Common Man* (1942), Carl J. Friedrich, a Harvard political scientist, presented a contrary view: "The basic, commonly felt needs permit the common man through his own sense of workmanship to evaluate a workmanlike performance [in government] without special intellectual equipment. Everyone knows when the shoe no longer pinches" (p. 265).

If this argument were sound, it would be unnecessary to examine and license physicians and lawyers because the common man could evaluate their workmanship. When medical care is poor, pain increases. Similarly, if a lawyer is incompetent, he loses too many cases. In both instances, the customer can tell "when the shoe no longer pinches." The service is performed before his eyes and he personally and directly senses the result. Yet I feel sure Professor Friedrich would not support any proposal to allow laymen, or their chosen representatives, to practice medicine or law.

The case for permitting non-experts to practice legislation and political administration is much weaker because it is much more difficult for the consumer to tell "when the shoe no longer pinches." If a government adopts an unsound tax, tariff, or educational policy, the resulting real cost or pain is much less likely to be immediately noticed by the voter than the pain resulting from bad medical care or legal advice. Moreover, a socially harmful law or administrative ruling may actually benefit many men, including those who have the most political influence. It is therefore more important to employ certified experts in government than in medicine or law.

SOCIAL PROBLEMS BECOME MORE COMPLEX AND NUMEROUS

Government by experts will be the next major stage in political evaluation in democratic states because social problems are becoming more and more complex and numerous.

Nearly everyone is aware that social problems have become more complex and more numerous during the past century, but only a few men, chiefly social scientists, realize how complex and numerous they have already become and how fast they are becoming more complex. I could give a great many examples of this, and any example could be given in great detail, but I shall offer only a few examples, and these very briefly.

Why Government by Experts Is Coming

The problem of how to regulate public utility rates arose in the United States about a century ago, when state authorities first began to control the rates charged by canal, railroad, and water companies. Since then the number of such utilities has increased steadily, many other industries have been declared to be public utilities, and the services rendered by each utility have multiplied.

Moreover, modern governments must now fix many prices directly, as well as regulate price determination by private utilities. Such price determination and regulation is an extremely complicated economic problem, one that very few voters and representatives of voters are qualified to solve. It is true that legislators have widely recognized this fact, have often restricted themselves to stating general pricing policies, and have turned over the function of detailed price regulation to boards, administrators, and courts. Because few legislators are economists, however, the general pricing rules they have enacted have usually been unsound and most of the men appointed to price-determining and price-regulating agencies have been unqualified. Furthermore, legislators themselves have often fixed prices, such as postal rates, directly.

Many democratic legislators, and all judges, have been educated as lawyers. Lawyers are as incompetent as surgeons to determine ideal utility rates. Only economists who have specialized in welfare price theory and are free to apply sound but unpopular economic principles can fix public utility rates properly.

The problem of how to raise money to cover the expenses of government is as old as government, but it is a hundred times as difficult now as it was a century ago. The expenditures of the American federal government are a thousand times as large as a century ago. There are six times as many people to be taxed and their money income per capita is several times as high. Moreover, the number of taxes has been greatly increased, and every tax law has become far more complex. Some tax laws are hundreds of pages long, and interpretive decisions fill many volumes each year.

Taxation greatly influences the location of industry, the choice of methods of production, the net earnings of workers, and many other economic factors. Only economists who have specialized in taxation are competent to devise a tax system that will maximize economic welfare. Voters and their representatives have made innumerable crude mistakes by approving new taxes that reduce, or obviously fail to maximize, economic welfare.

It is not only modern economic problems that are far too complex for intelligent treatment by voters and/or their representatives. Problems of public health, public education, defense, etc., likewise increasingly require consideration by experts. It is absurd that voters and legislators should choose textbooks, prescribe courses, reject vaccination or polio inoculation, and appropriate funds for submarines rather than airplanes. They are grossly unqualified to solve such complex professional problems.

All advanced countries have steadily expanded the scope of their operations, have begun to perform one new function after another, during the past two hundred years. In 1800, their cities did not even provide fire and police protection, and national governments did little more than provide courts of law and military defense. Now they operate railroads, air lines, coal mines, steel mills, atomic weapon plants, public utilities, satellite communication systems, and planetary exploration projects, as well as highway, education, and health-care systems. The acceptance of each new function increases the number and complexity of social problems, and all governments are sure to assume many more new functions during the next two hundred years. This will steadily increase the need for government by social scientists.

Martin Shubik, a Yale professor of economics, has recently emphasized that every increase in population, wealth, and knowledge makes political problems more complex:

> As the number of individuals, things, and concepts grows, it becomes more and more difficult to maintain a constant level of information. . . .
>
> If we believe that our political and economic values are

> based on the individual who understands principles, knows what the issues are, and has an important level of knowledge and understanding of his fellow citizens, then the 20th and 21st centuries pose problems never posed before. . . .
>
> In voting do we have criteria other than a blind faith in the "stolid common sense of the yeoman"? The growth in the size of the electorate and in the numbers and complexities of issues is only exceeded by the torrents of writings in which the public may be buried if it so chooses. In the jungle of municipal politics, even the well-educated and relatively more articulate part of the population is woefully under-informed.[2]

My prediction that the problems of government will continue to become more and more complex, even under socialism, was rejected by Karl Marx. He claimed that the achievement of socialism and communism will make these problems much less numerous and complex. It will transform government from the control of men into the administration of things because it will eliminate class conflict and the need to use government as an instrument of class rule. Like his other statements about how a socialist society would function, this too is brief and vague. Marx described in detail the path to socialism, but said little about how it would function.

One of his few other remarks on this topic, in *The German Ideology*, revealed a failure to appreciate the need for a division of labor and experts of any kind under socialism. "In the Communist society," he wrote, "society . . . makes it possible for me to do this today and that tomorrow, to hunt in the morning, to fish in the afternoon, to carry on cattle-breeding in the evening,"[3] and presumably to be any kind of public official on some other day.

Because Marx made little effort to support his claim that socialism would make political problems less complex, it is difficult to refute it. The achievement of full social ownership would certainly end the conflict between private-property owners and propertyless workers, but in a democratic socialist society there would still be many conflicts of interest. The workers in every area and/or industry would continue to be eager to raise their own real wages and improve their conditions of labor at the expense of other workers. The achievement of government by experts in a socialist society would largely free government officials from pressure by such special interests, but this would not make sociopolitical problems less complex; it would merely help enable officials to consider them more objectively, free from distracting and distorting political pressures.

Socialism will not substitute the administration of things for the government of men as Marx predicted. Rather it will add the administration of economic activities to the government of men. Of course, some major economic problems would be greatly clarified and simplified by the achievement of socialism. For instance, the organization of each industry as a pure monopoly would notably facilitate the formulation and enforcement of all desirable economic policies. On the other hand, such a reorganization of industry would itself be a complex new task, and the one-time simplification achieved by this reorganization would be but a single sharp decline in a long-run trend toward greater complexity of society and social problems.

The achievement of socialism will greatly simplify life for individuals—by assuring full employment, free medical care, nursery schools for children, honest advertising, and insurance against all risks—but it will not eliminate the factors that have long been making political problems more numerous and complex. Indeed, it will make such problems much more numerous and complex by increasing the functions of government.

Lenin, Marx's most famous and successful disciple, was more explicit in his rejection of the growing need for experts in government. According to Sheldon S. Wolin, Lenin believed that

> . . . the progressive simplification of [government] work would obviate the need for expert talents and place all functions within the reach of "every single individual." Since "democracy means equality," the development of organization could satisfy this criterion by breaking down complex jobs into simple operations.[4]

It is true, of course, that the division of labor simplifies many jobs, including many operations of government. But the division of labor has proceeded for centuries without reducing the demand for experts in business or government. Moreover, it does not simplify the individual problems faced by legislators and senior executives; it merely enables these men to specialize in certain kinds of problems and thus become more expert in dealing with them. And mere specialization in work does not enable laymen to deal with difficult professional problems—such as designing an ideal tax system or performing a brain operation—without professional training.

DECLINING INTEREST IN POLITICAL PROBLEMS

Government by experts is coming because in advanced countries the general public will become more and more willing to entrust the solution of political problems to experts because it will become less and less interested in such problems. As men in democratic countries become more prosperous, more secure, and more equal, the intensity of their interest in social problems will steadily decline.

The United States is very unlikely to achieve full government by experts before 2100, but by that time the average personal family income—which now doubles every forty to fifty years—should be well over $50,000 a year (in 1960 dollars). Moreover, the minimum personal income for a family of four will probably be over $30,000 a year. And every person and family will be insured against all major risks—birth of a defective child, insanity, criminal attacks, as well as against fire, accident, sickness, and unemployment.

The major functions of government are to make men increasingly prosperous and secure. As men become richer they become less interested in additional wealth. The marginal utility of income declines. And as men become more secure economically, their interest in additional social reforms designed to increase such security falls.

It is true, of course, that every advanced country now has a class of oppressed or unfortunate persons too worried about next week's food and shelter and/or too ignorant to take any interest in politics. This minority will for a time become increasingly interested and active in politics as its income and security grows. But all other classes will slowly lose interest as their incomes and security grow. And the lowest economic class will eventually follow their example.

All future social reforms that diminish gross discrimination—such as racial segregation, religious bias, and persecution of homosexuals—will reduce the intensity of interest in political activities in advanced societies. The alert victims of such discrimination are now especially interested in social reform, but this interest will wane as discrimination against them declines. And many reforms to reduce such discrimination will be adopted during the next two centuries.

Some new laws impose significant economic costs or losses on large numbers of men. For instance, prohibition compelled brewers and saloon keepers to seek new occupations and investments, often at a substantial personal sacrifice. One primary interest of most voters in democratic states is to avoid such costs. But all governments will increasingly adopt the practice of compensating individuals for significant losses caused by new laws and administrative rulings. Such compensation will become almost complete and universal before full government by experts is achieved. This development also will therefore steadily reduce public interest in elections and individual political policies.

One of the greatest personal risks in the modern world is the risk of death in war. It is quite likely that a world government able to drastically reduce this risk will be created before 2100, i.e., long before full government by experts is achieved. Any sharp reduction in the risk of property loss and personal injury from foreign military forces would significantly reduce public interest in political campaigns. Moreover, the removal of foreign policy decisions from national governments to an international or world government would probably have a similar effect, because it would sharply reduce the influence of an individual voter on such decisions and would make the relevant problems and policies both more remote and more complex.

A large share of existing public interest in political campaigns in democratic states results from sensational and overemotional stories in the press and in radio and television broadcasts. It is unfortunately easy to build circulation and/or win votes by getting large numbers of people excited about imaginary dangers such as the yellow peril, the red menace, and the spread of immorality and atheism in the universities. The continued growth of education should gradually reduce public fear of such largely imaginary dangers. Furthermore, the coming socialization of the major instruments of public communication—television, radio, and newspapers—will reduce the profit motive for sensationalism in news reporting. As a result, the public interest in political campaigns will decline. Even today the average voter is little interested in serious legislative proposals that promise only gradual solutions to complex and long-existing social problems.

It may seem that my prediction that public interest in political questions will decline for centuries is inconsistent with my prediction below that average intelligence and education will rise indefinitely. But during the last century public interest in agriculture and crop prospects has declined continuously in advanced countries, in spite of a steady rise in average education, because men have had less and less reason to worry about their abliity to get enough to eat.

Of course, "interest in politics" is an ambiguous term. What I am really predicting here is that men will become less and less interested in participating in politics, not in discussing or reading about social problems. In fact, men will become less interested in practicing politics even if they become more interested in discussing it. In the last hundred and fifty years men have become less and less eager to doctor themselves, but more and more interested in discussing recent advances in medical practice by experts.

Most defenders of democratic government have grossly exaggerated the degree of public interest in politics in normal times. It is easy for those few men who are deeply interested in social problems to overestimate such interest in other men.

In 1954 a very carefully conducted opinion survey of over a

thousand voters in Elmira, New York, found that these voters exhibited little sustained interest in politics. A 1961 survey of 525 registered voters in New Haven, Connecticut, yielded the same conclusion. Participation in local elections was found to be especially low.[5] The common belief that men are more interested in and better informed about local issues and candidates is false.

In 1966 the California State Committee on Public Education (SCOPE) hired the Field Research Corporation to survey California public opinion on education. They conducted 1001 in-depth interviews, and reported, among other things, that: (1) the great majority of Californians consider education the most important of all government functions, and (2) they are willing, for the most part, to delegate control over the performance of this vital function to experts because they consider themselves generally unqualified to make decisions regarding schools.[6]

In America, education is still largely under the control of local government, and school boards are usually elected in separate elections. If Americans are already willing to entrust this most important function to experts, they should eventually be willing to entrust less significant functions of government to experts.

POLITICIANS MUST PLAY POLITICS

Another reason why government by experts is coming is that politicians selected by voters are compelled to devote a large part of their time to winning and maintaining political support. For them, politics is a career, one which they cannot abandon while in office. They must continue to devote many hours to purely political chores—speaking tours throughout the country, conferences with fellow politicians, and the like—and this reduces sharply the amount of time and energy they can devote to handling legislative and/or administrative problems of government. Thus, even if politicians were as competent as social scientists in handling these problems, which they are not, they could not handle them nearly as well because they could not devote as much time to them.

Why Government by Experts Is Coming

In two apt analogies, Schumpeter compared the politician serving as the chief executive in a democratic state to "a horseman who is so fully engrossed in trying to keep in the saddle that he cannot plan his ride, or to a general so fully occupied with making sure that his army will accept his orders that he must leave strategy to take care of itself."[7]

Politicians not only devote a great deal of time to politics, they also give political considerations great weight when they write or consider new laws and appoint subordinate administrators. They are not free to do what they believe is in the national interest because they must worry constantly about winning and keeping political support. Thus in America the political leaders of one party usually attack and vote against sound reforms proposed by the other party merely because they are proposed by the other party. And many new laws and administrative rulings are tailored to the wishes of large campaign contributors.

After a legislator in a democratic state has played politics long and hard enough to get elected, and when he is not playing politics to ensure his reelection, he tries to get his pet measures considered and approved by the legislature. This requires a considerable expenditure of time on political bargaining, persuasion, and legislative strategy and tactics. Like bargaining over prices in a bazaar, bargaining over mutual legislative favors wastes many hours. The formation of a coalition or the conclusion of an agreement on log-rolling consumes much time because many different men must be persuaded to work together.

Political bargaining not only wastes a great deal of time; it also results in much harmful legislation. For instance, nearly all protective tariffs are due to such log-rolling. Each individual tariff injures the vast majority of voters, and alone may be unable to win legislative approval. Therefore, legislators desiring a tariff that will benefit their constituents must agree with other representatives desiring other tariff changes for similar reasons in order to secure a majority in the national legislature. But the usual result of such a combination of interests is a tariff bill which injures the nation. Log-rolling may be used to create or protect monopolies, uneconomic taxes, professional privileges, unjustified subsidies, and other undesirable laws and policies, as well as protective tariffs.

Under government by experts, log-rolling would be drastically reduced. Legislators would not represent different areas, occupational groups, or economic interests. They would look at all social problems from a national, not a local or occupational, point of view. Thus, there would be little need or opportunity for political log-rolling. Furthermore, all legislators would be social scientists carefully educated to seek and value the national interest, not the welfare of special interests. Before becoming politicians, democratic legislators have been carefully educated to promote the interests of private clients and employers, and have long experience in doing so. It would be hard for them to change suddenly into experts on and advocates of the public interest, even if this would further their political ambitions, which, of course, it would not.

In *The Public Philosophy* Lippmann wrote:

> With exceptions so rare that they are regarded as miracles and freaks of nature, successful democratic politicians are insecure and intimidated men. They advance politically only as they placate, appease, bribe, seduce, bamboozle, or otherwise manage to manipulate the demanding and threatening elements in their constituencies. The decisive consideration is not whether the proposition is good but whether it is popular—not whether it will work and prove itself but whether the active, talking constituents like it immediately (p. 27).

Unfortunately, nearly all the "active, talking constituents" are active in the promotion of some special interest, not of the public interest.

GOVERNMENT BY EXPERTS IS SUPERIOR TO DICTATORSHIP AND MONARCHY

It has long been recognized that dictators have some important advantages over democratic rulers. They can resist strong special interests, make long-run plans, carry out unpopular but

Why Government by Experts Is Coming

beneficial reforms, reach more rapid decisions, and make broader use of expert advice. All of these advantages would also be enjoyed by the top executive of a state governed by experts. And the latter would suffer few if any of the major disadvantages of government by dictators.

The chief disadvantage is that many dictators are incompetent because they lack the native ability, education, and experience required to make an able ruler. The great majority of dictators in the twentieth, as in the nineteenth, century have been military officers. Their chief asset has been military power. Professional military training does not produce able statesmen, politicians, or social scientists. Franco, Horthy, Pétain, and Perón illustrate this general rule.

Another important class of dictators, the Fascist demagogues, have proven even less competent. They have been overemotional, anti-intellectual, and poorly educated. Neither Hitler nor Mussolini ever attended a university.

It is noteworthy that most military and Fascist dictators have been, and will probably continue to be, strongly biased against social science, social reform, higher education, and intellectuals. As a result, they usually ignore or neglect expert advice, antagonize the intellectuals, and block or retard normal social progress.

Communist dictators have been more successful than military and Fascist dictators because they have accepted and applied some advanced social theories developed by able social thinkers. One of their greatest achievements has been a vast expansion of education, especially professional university education. Moreover, it is well to bear in mind that Communist dictators rule countries which, except for Czechoslovakia, had never been democratic. Nevertheless, Communist dictatorship, a transitional form of government, shares the chief disadvantages of dictatorship. Stalin was neither an able nor a benevolent ruler!

Another major disadvantage of dictatorship is that most dictators try to remain dictators indefinitely. There is rarely any agreed and observed procedure for peacefully replacing one dictator with another. It is a great advantage of democracy that it assures a peaceful replacement of one administration by another. A sound system of government by experts would also have this advantage. The chief executive would be periodically chosen by fellow experts or the national legislature, and made responsible to them. Moreover, social scientists chosen in this manner would understand the benefits of peaceful replacement of national leaders, and therefore would be much less likely to try to prevent their own peaceful replacement.

Aristocratic and oligarchic governments have often attempted to solve the problem of peaceful transfer of power from one ruler to another by making political office hereditary. But when any office is hereditary, it may be inherited by a fool, and is usually inherited by a very ordinary, mediocre person. A dynasty is normally founded by a relatively able man, but his sons and grandsons are usually less and less able. Scientists call this decline "regression to the norm," and, in the absence of eugenic control, it seems to be inevitable. It explains why, for instance, the kings and queens of England have for centuries been much less able than their prime ministers. The latter were selected in part for their ability to lead men; the former were not.

THE GROWTH OF KNOWLEDGE

The next reason why the rise of government by experts selected by experts in government is inevitable is that the continued growth of knowledge will make expert government both more desirable and more desired. Each of these two points is important.

The growth of knowledge has been accelerating for at least a thousand years, and is much faster today than ever before. It will continue to accelerate for many years to come. We live in the midst of a veritable explosion of knowledge, especially of knowledge concerning personal and social problems and behavior.

Every increase in the sum total of human knowledge makes it more difficult for one man to master all of it, even in a single field of knowledge. As a result, professionalization and specialization among professional workers has long been growing and will continue to grow indefinitely. And even highly educated specialists become less and less competent to deal with problems outside their specialty. The solution of social and political problems already requires specialized professional knowledge, and the relative advantages of using such knowledge will increase steadily as such knowledge grows.

The social sciences are among the newest and least developed of all the sciences. Political economy, the oldest, is less than two hundred years old. Adam Smith, generally recognized as its founder, published the *Wealth Of Nations* in 1775. And sociology, the youngest major social science, was founded by August Comte some seventy years later.

The creation of the social sciences came later, and their development has proceeded more slowly, than that of the natural sciences, because the problems of social science are more difficult, because powerful vested interests—religious, economic, political, and traditional—have feared and opposed the advance of social science, and because social inventions are not nearly as profitable to businessmen or as useful to military leaders as the numerous inventions made possible by research in the natural sciences.

Social problems are relatively complex because they require consideration of the effects of social change on millions of men who differ very widely in many important respects. Moreover, scientific experimentation with social forces or inventions is usually much more difficult, expensive, and time-consuming than such experimentation with natural forces and mechanical or chemical inventions.

The application of scientific method to social problems has always been firmly opposed by powerful vested religious and economic interests because it threatens many important religious and economic dogmas. For instance, the study of population problems has already led most social scientists to reject religious dogmas on birth control and abortion. And the advance of economics has helped to create wide political support for progressive income taxes, social insurance, and public ownership of utilities, all of which are, or were, opposed by most businessmen.

In spite of such opposition, the social sciences have made great progress during the last two centuries. One notable evidence of this progress is that a majority of the most respected social scientists already agree on a large number of desirable social policies and reforms, including those mentioned above.

The number of social scientists has increased a hundredfold during the past two hundred years and will increase rapidly in the next two hundred. Moreover, the funds available for research in social science will grow much faster than the number of social scientists. By 2100 every advanced government will spend as much, proportionately, on such research as the United States now spends on weapons research. This vast expansion in social science personnel and research funds will enable social scientists to create more and more reliable and verifiable principles of social science, which will greatly increase public confidence in the social sciences.

The advance of social science will make the principles of applied social science less and less controversial. By 2200 the basic principles of social engineering will be almost as noncontroversial as those of mechanical engineering today. The public will have nearly as much confidence in social engineers as in civil and mechanical engineers.

In an 1829 letter to d'Eichtal, John Stuart Mill wrote:

> They [the St. Simonians] have held out as the ultimate end towards which we are advancing, and which we shall one day attain, a state in which the body of the people, i.e., the uninstructed, shall entertain the same feeling of deference and submission to the authority of the instructed, in morals and politics, as they at present do in the physical sciences. This, I am persuaded is the wholesome state of the human mind. . . .[8]

THE GROWTH AND DEMOCRATIZATION OF EDUCATION

The vast contemporary expansion of secondary and higher education in advanced countries is rapidly creating a public that appreciates the benefits of higher education and the unusual

Why Government by Experts Is Coming

ability of the experts produced by it. This expansion began in America, has spread to Europe, the U.S.S.R., and Asia, and will continue indefinitely. By 2050 all adults in advanced democratic states will be secondary school graduates, and 20 to 40 percent will be university graduates. Such electorates will become increasingly willing to entrust ever more functions of business and government to highly educated experts.

The mere expansion of secondary and higher education will make such education more and more democratic. Moreover, many measures designed to democratize higher education will be adopted. In the not distant future, nearly all gifted working-class children in advanced states will receive a professional education. As long as experts come largely from the upper and the upper-middle class, as they do now in capitalist countries, working-class voters will distrust government by experts. But as the number of experts coming from lower-class families steadily increases, and eventually becomes a majority, this lower-class distrust will gradually diminish.

One important result of the growth of education is that experts are becoming more numerous and influential. In every advanced society, the number of experts or professionals has been steadily increasing for at least a century, and the rate of increase is more rapid today than ever before. This alone is bound to increase the political influence of experts and public support for more government by experts. No class of men is more likely to appreciate the social advantages of government by experts in government than experts themselves. And they influence votes and public opinion far more than the average non-expert.

It is intellectuals, not workers or proletarians, who constitute the most progressive class in any advanced country. They invent the new tools that revolutionize methods of production. And they invent or create the new ideologies and scientific theories that guide human reaction to changes in the methods of production. Voltaire, Rousseau, Locke, Bentham, Marx, and the Mills were intellectuals, not workers. Government by experts will be achieved as a result of reform campaigns led by such intellectuals. And they will succeed because other intellectuals have previously created the new tools—books, libraries, social science, universities—that permit, and indeed require, the development of government by experts.

EUGENIC REFORM

Another reason why expert government is coming is that radical eugenic progress is inevitable. Public confidence in social science and in government by social scientists will grow because future eugenic reforms will notably increase the average native intelligence of voters. During the twenty-first and twenty-second centuries, all advanced countries will initiate and/or continually expand eugenic programs which, by 2200 will raise their average intelligence quotient by 20 to 50 points above the 1967 level.

This rise in I.Q. will greatly increase the benefits from education, which in turn will increase both the ability of experts and public confidence in them. The more intelligent and educated the man, the more he appreciates the merits of specialized professional education and its products, the experts.

Furthermore, the rise in average I.Q. will greatly increase both the number of scientific geniuses and public willingness to support scientific research on social problems, which in turn will speed up the advance of the social sciences. And the more these sciences advance, the greater will become the benefits of government by experts in social science.

The first eugenic programs will involve only sterilization of the least fit, and perhaps subsidies for additional procreation by the most fit. Later, all governments will promote artificial insemination with the sperm cells of very superior men, first by means of propaganda and then by subsidies. As a result, the rate of increase in average I.Q. will rise more and more rapidly.

It may be suggested that because the advance of both eugenic reform and higher education will make the average voter far more intelligent, they will reduce the need for government by experts. But the gap between the ability of the expert and that of the non-expert to solve social problems will steadily widen, and the ever more intelligent non-experts will increasingly realize this. They will therefore become more and more willing to entrust the solution of social problems to social scientists.

Eugenics is not the only possible means of sharply raising the native intelligence of men. Several experts on technological progress have predicted that within fifty years scientists will have developed drugs that can be safely used to raise the intelligence of voters. And they are also talking about dietary supplements as intelligence stimulants. Other less probable technological developments that might raise average I.Q.'s are genetic engineering (rearrangement of the chromosomes) and man-machine symbiosis (direct connection of the human brain with an electronic computer).[9]

I am very skeptical of such predictions for the near future, but they and others like them may well come true before 2200 and help to make government by experts more acceptable. Any invention or social reform which makes men more intelligent will make them more favorable to government by experts.

THE EQUALIZATION OF INCOMES

In every advanced country the growth of political democracy has brought about the rise of economic egalitarianism and socialism. When the poor are enfranchised, they begin to vote for a more equal distribution of wealth and income. As I have previously noted, so-called democratic states are only semi-democratic and will become more and more democratic for many more decades. They will therefore become ever more egalitarian and socialistic. But every egalitarian reform reduces the intensity of the class war or wars, and the result will in turn weaken opposition to government by experts. Most experts now come, and always will come, from upper-income classes (defined as those with incomes above the mean). The smaller the difference in income between upper- and lower-income classes, the less will be lower-class suspicion of and opposition to rule by experts.

Moreover, the coming equalization of incomes in democratic states will gradually reduce public interest in politics. One of the chief reasons wealthy men participate in political activities is to preserve their undeserved economic advantages, and many poor men do so primarily in order to reduce these advantages. As the poor gradually win this struggle, they will become less and less interested in politics. The rich also will lose interest as their advantages are reduced, and as they increasingly realize that they cannot restore them by political activity.

Relatively complete socialism will be achieved before full government by experts. It will drastically reduce political struggles over shares in national income by ending inheritance, by socializing industry, and by permitting scientific non-political determination of personal incomes. It will largely eliminate unearned personal income, the major cause of political controversy over income determination.

For instance, in this coming democratic socialist society, it will not be necessary to pay army officers much more than enlisted men. The many non-monetary rewards of military rank— officers' clubs, use of official cars, better uniforms, symbols of rank, the pleasure of command, public recognition and praise— will be more than sufficient to induce all potential officers to seek higher military rank. The growth of democracy and equality of opportunity during the last two hundred years has already radically reduced the difference between the pay of a general and that of a private. This trend will continue until generals are paid little more than privates.

Medical doctors now earn far more than army officers because doctors have to pay a high price for their education while army officers receive free room and board, and pay no tuition at West Point. Free or adequately financed education of doctors would soon eliminate this differential.

Incidentally, the custom of paying officers much better than enlisted men did not arise because officers were more productive at the margin than enlisted men, nor because salary differentials induced individual officers to work harder. The custom began and continued because the social classes that provided most officers dominated the state and were able to use state revenues to give higher pay and undeserved privileges to their sons. Before the French Revolution the untrained and incompetent sons of aristocrats often became officers at age fifteen and colonels before thirty. And in Britain military commissions were sold, like government bonds, long after 1789.

Much the same situation existed in both the Catholic Church and the Church of England. Bishops lived in palaces not because they were more productive than parish priests, or because they needed special financial inducements, but because they were aristocrats and were accustomed to live well at the expense of the public.

Finally, continuing equalization of personal income will make education more democratic. It will enable more superior children from poor families to go to college and secure a graduate degree. It will increase competition for such degrees and for success in life after graduation. By reducing the influence of family wealth and power, it will reduce lower-class opposition to government by experts. And, by increasing competition for education and promotion as an expert, it will steadily improve the quality of experts, and therefore the advantages of government by experts.

THE RISE OF SOCIALISM

The next major specific reason why government by experts is coming is that the inevitable continued growth of socialism will favor the rise of expert government.

For instance, socialists will force governments to adopt more and more effective measures to make personal incomes more equal. Incomes are certain to become more and more equal whether or not socialism grows—that is why I discussed this trend separately—but socialist governments will speed up this trend and carry it farther than any capitalist government could. They will gradually abolish both private ownership of capital goods and inheritance of great wealth, which in turn will radically reduce unearned income. They will also radically restrict monopoly profits and monopoly elements in high wages and salaries.

To reduce private ownership, socialist governments will gradually transfer more and more industries from private to public agencies and will organize them in ever larger firms. This process will reduce family control over business management and favor the selection of professionally trained managers and their promotion on the basis of demonstrated ability. Nepotism has already been drastically reduced in those giant capitalist firms whose managers have taken over control from the owners. Such firms are an example of what will become universal under full socialism.

In addition, the rise of socialism will further weaken the spoils system and nepotism in politics. It will eliminate both the need for campaign funds and the ability of individuals to make large campaign contributions. Thus it will become unnecessary to appoint large campaign contributors to high political office. And low political offices will cease to be attractive and sought after because socialist governments will provide suitable jobs for all, regardless of which party wins the election.

Finally, the conclusive victory of socialism will end the need for property owners to dominate the government in order to preserve their vested interests. Capitalists have long distrusted or feared intellectuals and experts because the latter are less convinced of the need for the preservation of private ownership and nepotism. The eventual elimination of private ownership and inheritance will end this reason for opposition to government by experts.

James Burnham defines socialism as "a free and classless society" and claims that because every society must have a ruling class the achievement of socialism is impossible. To meet this criticism, socialists need only admit that there would be a non-hereditary ruling class in a socialist society.

A socialist society could not abolish classes based on ability, education, thrift, or economic function because men will always differ widely in these respects, but it could and would radically reduce or eliminate social classification based on inherited titles or wealth. That is what sensible socialists mean when they claim that socialism would create a classless society.

THE HIGH COSTS OF DEMOCRATIC ELECTIONS

A further reason why political democracy will be succeeded by expert government is that democratic elections are very expensive. Professor Heard, the leading American authority on such expenses, reports an estimate of $200 million for all cash outlays for nominating and electing local and national political officials in the United States in 1964.[10] This total does not include the public costs of conducting elections, estimated at one dollar per vote before World War II,[11] or the public costs of registering voters, which are now almost one dollar per registered voter. Altogether, such cash expenditures probably exceeded $500 million in 1968. Moreover, the value of the unpaid labor of volunteer campaign workers may have been even larger.

But these costs are only a small part of the total real cost of conducting democratic elections. By far the largest cost item is the enormous amount of time spent by potential voters in preparing themselves to vote by attending political meetings, reading political news and comments, watching political programs, listening to political radio broadcasts, and talking to friends about politics. If we estimate such time at thirty hours a year per average adult, and the value of such time at three dollars per hour, we get a national total for the United States of about $10 billion in 1968. The probable error in this estimate is much larger than the sum of the previous cost items, so they may be ignored. Ten billion dollars was about 1.3 percent of the United States national income in 1968.

Although presidential elections occur only once in four years in America, and with roughly equal frequency in other democratic countries, there are many other elections. In the United States the intervening Congressional elections probably cost at least half as much as the Presidential elections. And there are separate local elections—school board, county, city, special district—once or twice every year, in nearly all local areas. Thus it seems reasonable to estimate the average annual real cost of

American political campaigns and elections at about 1 percent of national income in the 1960s.

There would be some election costs in the country with the system of expert government suggested in Chapter 7. But they would be relatively insignificant because the number of voters would be reduced over 99 percent and the number of elections would be reduced by over 80 percent. Thus we may conclude that the elimination of democratic political campaigns in advanced countries would now save about 1 percent of the national income each year.

THE DECLINE OF RELIGION

The long decline in religious faith, which began several hundred years ago in Europe, will continue indefinitely in all nations, and will help to weaken opposition to government by experts. Religious people have always believed that social as well as personal behavior should be ultimately guided by religious or ethical principles, not by the principles of applied social science. Thus they prefer rule by religious politicians to rule by non-religious social engineers.

It is true, of course, that many social scientists are still religious, even when dealing with social problems. But there is an inescapable conflict between religious and scientific methods of thought, and social scientists are far less religious than laymen. Many are completely non-religious, and most religious social scientists try to be entirely scientific when working on social theories and problems. Those religious social scientists who still rely on holy books and revelation to solve social problems are frowned upon by their more orthodox colleagues and have little influence on the development or teaching of social science in non-religious institutions. They will have less and less influence as the years go by. That is one reason why many religious people will oppose the rise of government by experts. But their influence will decline very greatly during the centuries before such government becomes a serious political issue.

Most religious leaders and politicians in advanced countries now welcome the advice of technical experts because they know that such advice can always be rejected. What they are certain to oppose is granting the right of final decision on social policies to social scientists.

WORLD GOVERNMENT

For reasons which I have stated more fully elsewhere,[12] I believe that a strong world government or empire will be created before government by experts is achieved in any state. This world government will be dominated by one or more advanced states who, even if themselves democratic, will be unwilling to create political democracy in the world government because the population of backward nations is far larger and much less educated than the population of advanced states. But the dominant state or states will soon be willing to allow some foreign experts to participate in the central as well as the regional government of the world. This will permit all the peoples of the world to share increasingly in world government without endangering the success of such government by subordinating it to the whims and prejudices of voters in backward countries.

I have argued earlier that even in the most advanced countries the great majority of voters are incompetent as voters. All such arguments apply much more strongly in backward states. The gulf between expert and lay opinion is far wider in the latter than in the former countries. Thus government by experts will be relatively more advantageous in a world state than in the United States.

I also noted earlier that the creation of a successful world government would reduce public interest in politics by making all men more secure both in life and property. It will reduce fear of military attack and conquest in all nations. This in turn will reduce political tension and interest in politics within all nations, which will make men more willing to entrust government to experts in government. It is easy to excite the average voter by playing on his fear of foreign espionage or attack, but much more difficult to interest him in domestic social problems.

A SUMMARY OF THE RELEVANT EFFECTS OF LONG-RUN SOCIAL TRENDS

In my recent book, *The Next 500 Years* (1967), I described and illustrated thirty-one major general social trends, most of them centuries old, which will continue for centuries more. I have already explained how several of them will favor the rise of government by experts. Most of the others will also favor, though less strongly, the growth of government by experts. To support and elaborate this claim, I shall now review and comment on all thirty-one trends individually. This will involve some slight duplication of previously stated arguments for government by experts, but this repetition will clarify and summarize them.

1. *The growth of population* will promote the development of government by experts because it will make social problems more complex, and therefore more difficult for non-experts to understand. Moreover, every increase in population increases the advantages of a more intensive division of labor. It also increases both the number of scientific geniuses and the funds devoted to scientific research, both of which effects in turn speed up the accumulation of scientific knowledge which experts can make use of.

2. *The growth of scientific knowledge* is stimulated by the first trend but would continue in its absence. The steady growth of knowledge will help to bring about the rise of government by experts because every increase in the amount of knowledge widens the intellectual gap between the expert and the non-expert, and therefore increases the benefits from expert advice and management.

3. *The relative growth of scientific research* speeds up the growth of knowledge and also increases the proportion of the population engaged in scientific research. As noted earlier such persons are more likely to appreciate experts and expert opinion than the average man; a relative increase in their numbers will therefore increase public support for government by experts.

4. *The relative growth of education* will greatly increase the

relative numbers of both educators and well-educated persons, who will be much more likely than other men to appreciate and support government by experts.

5. *The democratization of education* will increase support for expert government because it will increase the proportion of experts who come from the lower social classes. Workers are now justifiably suspicious of many social scientists because the latter come almost entirely from above-average-income families and retain many social biases and prejudices due to their class origin.

6. *The decline of religion and superstition* will favor the rise of government by experts because, as noted earlier, nearly all religious people fear the influence of science and scientific experts. The decline of religion will make men more tolerant and more appreciative of expert scientific opinion in every field, including government.

7. *The growth of social control over social trends* will increase the need for government by experts because social control over social trends will become increasingly complex and difficult. Every expansion of government control over personal and social behavior creates new problems calling for more expert advice and management.

8. *The rationalization of all social policies* will also, and for the same reason, increase the need for experts in government. Experts know much more about such rationalization than do ordinary voters or non-expert politicians.

9. *The spread of birth control* will indirectly aid the rise of expert government because it will raise average real incomes, which will favor all but one of the trends discussed above—obviously it will not increase population—as well as others discussed below. For instance, it will speed up the improvement and democratization of education by reducing the number of children to be educated.

10. *Eugenic progress* will substantially raise the average native intelligence of the world population. As previously noted, this result in turn will make all education and scientific research more productive, which will speed up the growth of knowledge

and create a world population much more likely to appreciate the many advantages of government by experts in government.

11. *The rise in real wages* will promote all of the major trends discussed above except perhaps the growth of population—and most of those mentioned below. For instance, it will permit ever larger expenditures on education and research in the social sciences. It will also gradually reduce public interest in political problems because it will make men more content with social conditions and trends.

12. *The growth of leisure* is the first item in this list that does not clearly favor the rise of government by experts in government. Indeed, it might be plausibly claimed that as leisure increases men will become more eager to participate in political activities. But this one trend could not offset more than a small part of the effects of all the other trends noted here.

13. *Urbanization* will long continue to increase the complexity of social life and problems, which will increase public demand for expert government.

16. *Specialization.*

17. *Professionalization.*

Items 16 and 17 both include the rise of government by experts because such experts would be both specialists and professional men.

18. *The increase in the scale of production.*

19. *The growth of monopoly.*

Items 18 and 19 are both helping to bring about ever-increasing government regulation and ownership of industry, which make the political problems of a mixed economy increasingly complex. On the other hand, once socialism has been fully achieved, any further continuance of these trends would simplify the problems of managing industry.

20. *Centralization of control.*

21. *Collectivization.*

Like Items 18 and 19, the trends of Items 20 and 21 will increase and complicate the functions of the rulers of an advanced mixed economy, but, after all industry has been collec-

Why Government by Experts Is Coming

tivized, further centralization of control might simplify the problems of managing industry.

22. *The rise of meritocracy* includes the rise of government by experts, which is political meritocracy.

24. *The decline in income differences* will reduce opposition to government by experts because it will reduce lower-class envy and distrust of the upper class, from whom most experts in government now come.

25. *The relative growth of free distribution of economic goods* will have the same effects for the same reasons.

26. *The reduction of all personal economic risks* will diminish public interest in political problems and thus make the public more willing to relinquish control over political policies.

27. *Growing paternalism.*

28. *Growing humanitarianism.*

Items 27 and 28 will both require increased state control over private conduct, which will increase the number of complex problems of government and intensify the need for government by experts.

None of the six major trends predicted in *The Next 500 Years* but not discussed above—industrialization, automation, the advance of feminism, the growth of intergroup relations, cultural homogenization, and the growth of personal freedom—would hinder the rise of government by experts. Indeed, it is more likely that some of them would make the problems of government more complex and thus strengthen the case for government by experts. In summary, the great majority of the thirty-one principal social trends likely to continue during the next two or three centuries will probably tend to favor the rise of government by experts, and one only, the growth of leisure, might possibly hinder it.

4
A Critical Review of the Case for Political Democracy

Having stated in detail the reasons why the rise of government by experts in government, choosen by their fellow social scientists, is inevitable, I now propose to consider the arguments against this prediction. These arguments will be divided into two classes, the constructive arguments for democratic government, the most popular and likely alternative form of government in advanced countries, and the negative arguments against government by experts. Because some arguments may be stated either as arguments for democracy or as arguments against expert government, my classification is debatable, and may involve some duplication, but repetition in a different form may clarify these arguments. The present chapter is devoted to the constructive arguments for democratic government; the following, to arguments against government by experts.

One of my chief reasons for stating and criticizing here the conventional arguments for democracy is that I have been unable to find any comprehensive statement of the arguments against government by experts. This possible future form of government has received so little serious support that few men who would oppose it have thought it worthwhile to state their arguments against it. But most arguments in favor of democratic government imply more or less clearly that expert government would be less desirable, and many writers have stated such arguments. I shall therefore open my review of the case against expert government by reviewing and criticizing the chief relevant arguments in favor of democratic government.

THE MANY ARE WISER THAN THE FEW

One of the oldest arguments in favor of political democracy is that the people as a whole are wiser than any single man or any small group of men. Aristotle observed:

> The principle that the multitude ought to be supreme contains an element of truth. For the many . . . may very likely be better than the few good, . . . just as a feast to which many contribute is better than a dinner provided out of a single purse . . . although individually they may be worse judges than those who have special knowledge—as a body they are as good or better.[1]

Rousseau restated and elaborated this argument in his theory of the general will, which is always right.[2] And popular orators have often proclaimed that the voice of the people is the voice of God.

Taken literally, the reasoning behind such conclusions would seem to justify the use of democratic methods to treat disease and solve many other professional problems, but I think it was intended to apply only to non-professional problems. In other words, it assumes there is no profession or science of politics, and this has of course been true until very recently. The argument will lose its plausibility as the social sciences develop.

Moreover, it is not true that the opinion of the multitude is wiser than that of a small group of educated men on non-professional questions. A small group of able or educated men can usually render a wiser decision than any single member, but no further improvement results from a vast expansion in the size of the group, or from a lowering of the average ability and education of the group. As explained in the previous chapter, most voters are incompetent.

DEMOCRATIC RULERS LISTEN TO THE PEOPLE

Perhaps the most important argument for democratic government is that it assures that rulers will listen to the people, and, on most important issues, will adopt the most popular policies, whether or not they are the best. Democratic rulers must be popular to be elected, and they must adopt many popular policies in order to assure their reelection. They can often ignore popular opinion on minor issues, and occasionally on major issues, but they must adopt enough popular policies to keep a majority of voters reasonably satisfied with their performance.

Jeremy Bentham, a pioneer advocate of political democracy, stated this argument as follows:

> It is only in so far as the members of this House are in fact *chosen,* and from time to time *removable* by the free suffrages of the great body of the people, that there can be any adequate assurance, that the acts done by them, are in conformity to the sense and wishes of the people.[3]

Why should governments conform to the sense and wishes of the people? Some democrats have argued that the people as a whole are the best judges of national policies and interests. I think this claim is unjustified. But there is a much better reason why governments should adopt popular policies, namely that this greatly reduces the danger of riots, uprisings, and civil wars.

DEMOCRACY REDUCES THE DANGER OF RIOTS AND REVOLUTION

In a political democracy, ballots replace bullets as a means of settling political disagreements. In an undemocratic country, those who oppose the government often have both enough votes and enough bullets to overthrow it, but they must use bullets. In a democratic country, they can use votes instead of bullets, and the use of votes is far less costly, far less socially harmful. The American Civil War lasted for four years, killed some six hundred thousand men, and did enormous material damage. It occurred because the American people, especially those of the southern states, had not yet accepted the principle of democratic government. The Spanish Civil War of 1936-39 was even more costly in lives and property, and also occurred because many Spaniards had not yet accepted the principle of democratic government.

If a political party cannot win enough votes to win a national election, it usually cannot overthrow the government by force. Thus a democratic election is a peaceful substitute for an attempt at violent revolution. It ordinarily enables the opposition to determine in advance their prospects of success in an armed revolt.

Of course there are exceptions to this rule, like the Spanish Civil War. But if the Spanish rebels had paid more attention to the previous election returns, they would have realized more clearly how popular the democratic government was, and how great would be the cost in lives and property of overthrowing it. Furthermore, if they had understood the nature of democratic government, they would have known that sooner or later Spanish conservatives would win an election and come to power peacefully.

The democratic system of government provides a tested and successful means of transferring political power from one group of men to another without a coup d'etat or revolution. A state ruled by a dictator or a junta is in constant danger of violent overthrow, and this danger becomes much greater whenever a dictator dies.

The argument that political democracy assures the peaceful creation of governments which are popular and legitimate, and therefore reduces the danger of riots and revolution, suggests one argument against government by experts, namely that such governments could not minimize public opposition and discontent. This argument will be answered in Chapter 5.

DEMOCRACY EQUALIZES POLITICAL INFLUENCE

Bentham suggested a purely utilitarian or welfare argument for political democracy. On an average, he asserted, every individual has an equal capacity for happiness and an equal desire for happiness. Thus, if most men seek, and are the best judges of, their own interests, national welfare is maximized when all men have equal political influence, and equal voting power is a prerequisite for equal political influence.[4]

This argument closely resembles the modern utilitarian argument for equality of personal income. Like the latter, it is based on the fact that the pleasure obtained from each successive unit of consumption or income is less than that obtained from the previous unit, which economists call the principle of diminishing utility.

Certain welfare economists have improved this argument for equal income by explaining that whether or not men do on the average have an equal capacity for happiness, the estimate that they do have an equal capacity is the most accurate and useful one we can make. It minimizes the average error in estimating individual capacities.

The most serious defect in the utilitarian argument for equal political power is the assumption that all or most men are the best judges of their own interest. This claim has often been used to justify economic individualism and laissez-faire, as well as to justify equal voting rights, but it is very controversial. I have already explained why I believe experts in government know the political interests of most men much better than the men themselves. Of course, I am really talking about the best political means of achieving ultimate personal ends, not the ultimate ends themselves, but this is what the term "interest" usually denotes in such arguments.

Another serious defect in this utilitarian argument is that it assumes that by equalizing voting rights we equalize political power. In fact, even when all adults can vote, the rich and/or able have far more political power per person than do the poor and/or inarticulate. Thus, the former can and do persuade democratic governments to favor them and neglect the poor, in spite of the fact that the latter may have an equal capacity for happiness. If personal incomes were equalized, men would gain an almost equal opportunity to influence the production and consumption of price goods so as to maximize their pleasure from such goods. But when voting rights alone are equalized, men do not gain equal influence over government policies and cannot maximize their welfare from such policies.

DEMOCRACY REPRESENTS ALL INTERESTS

Another, and closely related, argument in favor of political democracy is that because all men and all classes seek to achieve their own narrow goals, the goals of men who cannot participate in the selection of their rulers are likely to be neglected or ignored by these rulers. As James Mill lucidly explained:

> Whenever the interests of two sets of people are combined together in one concern, if the entire management is left to one, it is perfectly clear that this managing set will draw, by degrees, all the advantages to their own side, and throw all the disadvantages to the other: . . . [5]

This quotation may exaggerate the evils of class rule, but it is certainly correct in its main thesis. The aristocracy did abuse and exploit other classes under feudalism, as does the capitalist class in capitalist democracies. If undemocratic government enables some men, the ruling class, to oppress and/or exploit all other men, one obvious solution is to include all men in the ruling class, in other words, to establish a fully democratic government.

The chief fault in this argument is that it assumes that all men are equally able to participate or achieve representation in a democratic government. Even when such participation or representation is legally possible, important elements in the population are unable to achieve it because they are poor, badly educated, incompetent, misinformed, or neurotic. One great advantage of government by experts is that experts would give more consideration to the interests of these depressed or unfortunate groups than do politicians elected by all voting groups.

The argument that a democratic government represents all political interests suggests at least two possible arguments against government by experts: (1) that experts would ignore the desires and interests of some social classes or occupational groups, and (2) that these experts would favor their own personal, family, and professional interests and those of their colleagues most responsible for their election or appointment to high office. These are plausible and serious arguments. They will be discussed in the next chapter.

DEMOCRACY MAKES MEN FEEL FREE

It has often been claimed that the rise of political democracy helped to make men feel free, equal, and proud. Certainly the sudden enfranchisement of a former slave, serf, or other disfranchised citizen normally has such desirable effects. But this is primarily because the disfranchised were previously exploited and/or looked down on by the enfranchised, who claimed to be and were social superiors. There is little reason to believe that a long gradual process of transferring political power from representatives of the people to experts in government has made, or will make, the citizens of advanced countries feel less free, less equal, or less proud. They do not feel less free or equal when they give up self-medication and entrust their health care to experts. They will become increasingly aware that entrusting political functions to experts is as beneficial and liberating as entrusting their medical care to medical experts.

Even in the most advanced democracies there are large classes of men who still feel unfree, inferior, and ashamed, because they are unemployed, poor, or members of racial or religious minorities. The best way to make them feel free, equal, and proud is to achieve full employment, equalize personal incomes, and reduce discrimination. A government of experts would be able to approach these goals more rapidly and efficiently than a democratic government. When all men are well-to-do and incomes are almost equal, citizens will not feel humiliated or exploited by the assignment of political functions to experts paid little more than the average man.

In sum, the argument that the introduction of democratic government makes men feel free, equal, and proud is a valid argument for supporting a change from feudal or dictatorial rule to democratic rule, but is not a valid argument against the coming change from democratic to expert government in affluent, egalitarian countries.

DEMOCRACY EDUCATES THE PUBLIC

In his *Representative Government* (1860) John Stuart Mill, an able proponent of political democracy, claimed as a major advantage of such government that it would educate the general public by inducing more of them to read, listen to, or participate in discussions of political issues:

> A person must have a very unusual taste for intellectual exercise in and for itself, who will put himself to the trouble of thought when it is to have no outward effect, or qualify himself for functions which he has no chance of being allowed to exercise (chap. 3, p. 3).

If a man is not allowed to vote, he will not bother to learn how to vote wisely.

Undoubtedly the rise of democracy has increased public interest in political issues, although most of the rise in such interest may have resulted from growth in real incomes, leisure, and education. There has been a similar, perhaps greater, rise in public interest in medicine and in science among persons who do not practice medicine or science.

Furthermore, the argument that we should allow all adults to practice applied social science, or to choose those who practice it, in order to increase their interest in, and knowledge of social science is, or will soon become, almost as unsound as the argument that we should allow all adults to practice medicine, or choose those who do so, in order to increase their interest in and knowledge of medicine. As soon as the development of social sciences produces social scientists who know much more about political problems than laymen, these experts should be entrusted with the function of government, for the same reason that doctors should be entrusted with the function of medical care.

Finally, the great majority of men would benefit much more from increased knowledge of how to handle their own personal problems than from increased knowledge of how to vote intelligently. At least this would be true if government were in the hands of experts. And until we place government in expert hands, the time and money devoted to preparation for intelligent voting is a major cost of democratic government.

Because knowledge is already so vast and is growing so rapidly, men cannot spend some time studying social science and current political problems without spending less on other studies. And some other studies are very rewarding. For instance, if men spent less time reading political news and more time reading medical news, many more of them might cease smoking cigarettes and eating butter, and thereby prolong their productive lives by five to ten years.

DEMOCRACY MAKES MEN MORE MORAL

Mill claimed that assignment of the function of government to competent but undemocratically chosen rulers would be morally as well as intellectually harmful to the public: "Their moral capacities are equally stunted. Wherever the sphere of action of human beings is artificially circumscribed, their sentiments are narrowed and dwarfed in the same proportion." To a positivist (like the author), the term "moral" is always senseless or superfluous. Moreover, if meaningful, this argument would apply to all rules that restrict professional or skilled work to licensed practitioners. Yet such restrictions are widespread, and steadily increasing in number, and have rarely if ever been criticized for stunting human moral capacities. The rise of government by experts in government will be a further extension of the practice of restricting professional work to licensed professional men.

Mill also argued that democratic government is morally superior because it makes men "self-dependent" instead of dependent on the actions of undemocratic rulers, however benevolent and able the rulers may be. But it would be equally reasonable to argue that self-medication is morally preferable to medical care by a physician because self-medication makes one "self-dependent" or independent.

Mill's use of such unsound arguments in favor of political democracy suggests how strongly he desired democratic government, and how easy it is, even for a brilliant and relatively scientific thinker, to accept and use unsound arguments for a much desired reform.

Experience in any kind of decision-making improves one's ability to make those decisions. There is no distinct field of moral decisions in which experience is more helpful or more needed. And most political decisions are not even popularly classed as moral decisions.

DEMOCRACY FAVORS THE RISE OF THE MOST ABLE

David Spitz has claimed that political democracy is the best form of government because it favors the rise of the most able men to high political office:

> Where equality of citizenship and of opportunity are assured, the inequalities that are inherent in men's natures or personalities are given free reign to exert an unequal impact on political and social affairs. Unequal men are enabled to hold unequal political office, exercise an unequal political influence, and enjoy unequal political status, all in accordance with their varying abilities.[6]

This claim is explicitly based on the unrealistic assumption that equality of opportunity has already been achieved. However, I have predicted an ever closer approach to such equality. Thus this unrealistic assumption does not invalidate Spitz's claim, at least as a prediction, and my thesis is a prediction.

The major defect in this argument for democracy is that Spitz implies that equal competition for the votes of all adults does or will lead to electoral victories for the most able candidates. This implication is quite unjustified. Hitler won his way to power primarily by winning electoral victories. The vast majority of political observers are aware that democratic elections do not usually result in victory for the ablest potential candidate. And it is not inequality of opportunity among candidates, but the low average ability of voters that is chiefly responsible for this.

It is true that democratic rulers have been abler than contemporary aristocratic rulers, but it is not true that the average voter in a democracy can choose among candidates as wisely as social scientists could. Furthermore, a larger number of able men would become candidates if they knew the electorate was small and highly educated in social theory and practice.

Spitz asserts that under political democracy "the inequalities that are inherent in men's natures or personalities are given free reign to exert an unequal impact on political and social affairs." This desirable result would be much more fully achieved under government by experts than under government by representatives of the people because experts are better judges of government officials.

THE NATURAL RIGHTS ARGUMENT

Another possible argument for democratic government is that every man has a natural right to participate in electing those who govern his country. Because it is easy to assert that men have any natural right, and impossible to prove that they do not, such arguments have been widely used. But they are all literally senseless because no one knows what they mean. The mere fact that it is impossible to conceive of any method of disproving that a natural right exists proves that any claim that such a right exists is nonsensical, i.e., unsupportable by sensory observation. One can prove or disprove the claim that an alleged legal right exists by studying the relevant laws and court decisions, but there is no conceivable way of proving that any natural right exists.

The term "natural rights" is a typical senseless philosophic term. It has no determinable referent. Men use it—like the terms "moral," "just," and "ethical"—to try to transform their personal prejudices into factual truths. When a writer claims men have a natural right to live, to be free, or to vote, he merely shows his personal approval of such desires or privileges; he does not state a verifiable fact about them.

This argument for democracy implies, of course, an argument against government by experts, namely that such government would violate a natural right, the right to vote. This argument is senseless for the reasons given above.

DEMOCRACY CAN BE GREATLY IMPROVED

One final important argument for political democracy deserves consideration. It is possible to recognize that democratic government, as now practiced, has many faults and still claim that most or all of these faults could be eliminated without abandoning the basic principles of democracy. For instance, a supporter of democracy may concede that democratic politicians must now spend too much time raising campaign funds and must grant special favors to large campaign contributors, and may then point out that these evils could be drastically reduced by providing for government financing of political campaigns. Likewise he could concede that democratic legislators now perform many functions that should be turned over to experts, and then argue that these functions could, and perhaps will, be turned over to experts without abandoning any essential principle of democratic government. Many other illustrations could be given.

I think this argument for democracy has a good deal of merit. Democratic governments will certainly be steadily improved. For that reason, I have consistently striven to avoid criticizing democratic government for obvious but remediable or non-essential defects. Furthermore, in praising government by experts, I have tried to stress merits that could not be achieved even by an ideal democratic government.

5

The Chief Arguments Against Government by Experts

The next two chapters are devoted to a statement of the arguments against government by experts and my response to these arguments. In this chapter I shall deal with the chief possible individual arguments. In the following chapter I shall review the surprisingly varied briefs against the idea of expert government or political meritocracy offered by each of the principal explicit critics of these ideas.

The proposal of government by experts, i.e., by social scientists chosen by social scientists, is so new, so incompletely formulated, and so little known that it has as yet provoked very little serious discussion or criticism. In this chaper I shall therefore state and answer some possible but unused arguments, as well as those actually used against this and similar proposals.

As noted earlier, religious and philosophic thinkers are unable or reluctant to accept the thesis that social policies should be determined by social scientists in a purely scientific manner because they believe that religious revelations and/or non-empirical ethical principles should guide or influence social behavior. I shall not review in detail here the religious and philosophic arguments against full reliance on science because they have been repeatedly and competently stated and refuted elsewhere. But I believe religious and philosophic motives are behind many of the scientific arguments discussed below, in other words, that many of these arguments are rationalizations of unstated, and often unconscious, religious and philosophic biases. Of course, ethical arguments have been openly stated by some of the critics of expert government. I shall answer these critics without attempting a full discussion of the reasons why all such arguments are false or senseless.

EXPERTS WOULD ENRICH THEMSELVES

Perhaps the most obvious possible major objection to government by experts in government is that such experts would favor and enrich themselves, their relatives, and their supporters at the expense of the nation. All past ruling classes and groups have done so, and some writers claim that this evil would be serious even in a socialist meritocracy.

The men who originated, or at least did the most to popularize, this argument—Mosca, Pareto, Nomad, and others—taught that every society is ruled by an exploiting elite. Because their theory applies to all societies, it does not justify a rejection only of government by experts. If we accept their theory, the basic point at issue is not whether expert rulers would enrich themselves and their families and followers but whether they would do so more or less than democratic politicians.

Because experts in government would not have to raise large campaign funds or curry favor among various groups of businessmen, the need for and temptation to bribery and economic favoritism would be far less under government by experts than under modern democratic government. Moreover, experts now in public employment—public health doctors, military officers, government engineers, economists, *et al.*—have an excellent record in these respects, at least in advanced countries. Bribery and corruption are much more common among elected officials than among appointed experts. And several scientific studies have shown that the most able (highest I.Q.) and/or best educated people are the most honest and public-spirited.

Although experts would be less prone to corruption and exploitation than any previous ruling elite, they would tend to favor unduly their own special interests unless prevented from doing so. But there are many ways of minimizing such favoritism, and the class that would be favored would be very small and very worthy.

The Chief Arguments Against Government by Experts

For instance, a law or constitution unchangeable by expert rulers could provide that such rulers should not be paid more than twice the average salary of all workers. Or a special body of representatives elected by all adults could be created to pass and enforce such laws, and perhaps certain other fundamental laws controlling the organization and performance of a government of experts.

In any case, all advanced countries will become largely or completely socialistic and egalitarian before they achieve government by experts. Thus political rulers and senior executives of all kinds will become accustomed to relatively low salaries, probably less than three times the national average, and all large incomes from private property will be eliminated, under democratic government. This will drastically reduce the temptation and opportunity for bribery of public officials and for high living by them when expert government is achieved.

High pay for men in high position began when nearly all such men came from a small aristocratic class in complete control of state and church. This custom was naturally carried over into newer professions as these professions became suitable occupations for the younger sons of noble families. The modern theory that men in high position need higher pay to induce them to accept these positions is merely an apologetic rationalization of a custom established to serve an entirely different purpose, namely to enable the disinherited sons of aristocratic families to live like gentlemen. It is true, of course, that in bourgeois societies high pay for high position rarely serves this original function. It is rather a reward for monopoly, for going to the best schools, for the right family contacts and influence, for unusual ability, and so on. But, whatever the explanation, the payment of relatively very high salaries as an inducement to accept or hold a high position is entirely unnecessary. The opportunity to exercise power is itself a more than adequate inducement to persuade able men to seek high positions.

The mere long continuance of the custom of paying men in high positions or prestige occupations much more than men in low positions or occupations has of course caused nearly all men to think that such income differentials are natural, normal, and inevitable, but such is not the case. All great social changes are gradual, as will be the rise of government by experts, but the further decline and eventual elimination of both large inter-occupational and inter-rank income differentials is inevitable. Because the rise of government by experts will also be gradual, these income differentials will not be high enough to create hereditary classes or to permit great differences in living standards when government by experts is achieved.

EXPERT GOVERNMENT WOULD BE UNPOPULAR

Another possible major argument against government by experts is that expert rulers chosen by social scientists would be unpopular, or at least would rarely if ever have as much popular support as democratically elected rulers. This argument undoubtedly has some merit. I do not think experts chosen by experts could be as popular as men like Eisenhower and Franklin D. Roosevelt. On the other hand, expert rulers should on the average be more attractive and popular than Coolidge and Hoover. Expert electors would surely be wise enough to give some consideration to personal charm in selecting a chief executive.

The popular support of elected leaders is now largely created by opinion-forming agencies—newspapers and radio and television stations. If it is considered desirable, these agencies could be used more effectively to build popular support for expert rulers and, much more important, for the system of government by experts. For instance, Russian opinion-forming agencies made the unattractive Stalin very popular. Such organized adulation of national leaders can easily become excessive, but some may be desirable.

Scientific public-opinion polling, first tried in the 1930's, has been steadily improved since then. It can give public officials a much better idea of public opinion on individual political issues than democratic elections do. The top experts of a country governed by social scientists would surely know enough to make wide use of public-opinion polls and to refrain from actions they know to be so unpopular they would cause riots or excessive opposition.

C. A. R. Crosland has asserted that men do not now want to be governed by experts.[1] This is probably true today, and may long continue to be true, in democratic nations. But political democracy was equally unpopular and impractical two hundred years ago. I do not claim that government by experts is popular today in advanced countries. My thesis is that this form of government will become popular at some future time, probably before 2200.

All of the social trends that make such government inevitable will also steadily increase popular support for government by experts. As social problems become more complex, as the social sciences progress, as voters become better educated, and so forth, public respect for experts and public support for expert government is certain to increase.

EXPERTS KNOW HOW, NOT WHAT

A third major argument against government by experts is that experts are competent to tell us how things should be done, but not what should be done. Various reasons have been offered to support this argument. Theologians, moralists, and many writers who accept their dogmas claim that the problem of what to do is a moral problem that scientists cannot solve. Because I have criticized this claim in detail in another book, I wish to minimize discussion of it in this one, but some comments are necessary.

In his widely read book, *The Organization Man* (1956), William H. Whyte, Jr., stated this claim as follows:

> Let us assume . . . that a precise science of man is not a will-o'-the-wisp and that we are on our way to achieving it. We are left with the knotty problem. What do we do about good and evil, right and wrong? . . . a science of man could not freeze on one scheme of ethics . . . however, it would need some sort of ethics. How are we to determine just what they should be? (pp. 31-32)

This question reveals a deplorable ignorance of the development of philosophy and ethics since 1920. The logical positivists and analytic philosophers have repeatedly explained why all ethical principles are factually senseless and/or purely emotional, and therefore superfluous. To determine sound social policies, social scientists do not need to know what is ethically right or wrong. They only need to know what men want. The function of government, like that of the economic system is to maximize want satisfaction or welfare.

For over two thousand years moralists have been trying to discover and agree upon basic ethical truths, but they disagree more widely now than ever before. The reason is very simple. The methods they use reveal only personal prejudices and provide no means of determining which prejudice is true and which is false. Only science has methods of settling disputes, of verifying factual truth claims. Moral opinions depend on such factors as place and time of birth, parentage, and indoctrination. Only scientific truths are accepted throughout the world because only such truths can be verified by observation and experiment.

So-called moral principles that are verifiable are either false or superfluous, because all verifiable truths belong to some science. Unverifiable truths are literally senseless because they cannot be verified by sense data.

Certain writers claim that decisions as to what is to be done must be made by voters or their representatives. For instance, David Spitz has written: "The expert knows how to do something, not what is to be done. The latter is the effective range of everyman."[2] And Benn and Peters have said: "The essential skill of the expert is to suggest ways of solving problems: that of the statesmen, to see which suggestions the public would turn down."[3]

Such claims may be based partly on the belief that experts, especially those in the natural sciences and technology, have specialized so long and so narrowly that they have lost contact with practical problems of common people. This belief is exaggerated. All experts must face and solve personal and family problems, as well as those of their specialty. But it would certainly be unwise to assign top political functions to experts who are narrow specialists.

There are two chief possible answers to the secular claim that well-rounded experts, generalists in social science, do not know what is to be done, i.e., what the public wants done. First, men who become experts do not thereby lose their awareness of basic human instincts, wants, and goals. The expert is "everyman" as well as an expert. He does not need to be told by voters and their representatives that normal men want food, shelter, clothing, mates, children, security, and recreation. And he does not need to decide what kinds of food, shelter, and clothing should be produced.

In a well-run advanced capitalist or socialist economy consumers can determine what is produced and sold by buying more or less of each good. It is a function of government to preserve or increase such freedom of choice, not to determine what price goods consumers should consume.

Of course, a government must determine what free goods—free public services—should be produced, but in doing so it should rely on medical, educational, military, and other experts, not on voters. Most free goods have been provided free of charge chiefly because many consumers would not buy enough of them if they were sold for a price. Public education, free medical care, and social insurance are examples of such free goods. And appropriate experts are also more competent to determine "what is to be done" concerning other free public services, such as military and police protection.

The only ultimate goal of government should be to maximize welfare per citizen. This can be achieved by maximizing individual freedom of choice of jobs, occupations, places of residence, price goods, and leisure, and by relying on expert advice concerning the provision of free professional services.

The second answer to the secular claim that experts know how, not what, is that the political problems with which governments deal are not whether men should have such items as food and shelter, but how these universally desired goals can be achieved. All such practical problems fall within the effective range of experts, not of everyman.

Of course, the phrase "what is to be done" is ambiguous. It is easy to restate any problem as to how some goal can be achieved as a problem as to what should be done, but this should not obscure the real nature of political problems. *All practical political problems are problems of how some more general and ultimate end should be achieved.*

The argument that experts know how not what implies that those who rule democratic states now spend most of their time deciding what ought to be done, not how it is to be done. In fact, the opposite is true. For instance, over 90 percent of the content of new laws passed by the United States Congress deal with methods of achieving political ends. Instead of merely instructing the administration to achieve certain results—to improve education, health, social security, and military defense—the Congress writes laws containing millions of words prescribing precisely how such desired results shall be achieved. It even approves the promotion of higher military officers, chooses individual military weapons, locates individual military camps and hospitals, and in many other ways determines how desired national goals should be achieved. Obviously, it does not accept the claim that experts know how these goals can best be achieved.

It is noteworthy that few of the commonly professed goals or values of voters and politicians are ultimate ends. The most general and popular political goals—freedom, security, welfare, and progress—are very vague. That is one reason they are so popular! But most less general and more specific "values" are means to ends rather than ultimate social goals. For instance, men who believe that capitalism, private inheritance, social insurance, or socialism would maximize freedom or welfare often treat these means as intrinsically desirable ends. Most so-called personal and social "values" are really unjustified personal prejudices concerning means to achieve commonly desired, more ultimate ends. Thus there is no good reason why such "values" should influence social policies, except the fact that any government must be careful not to arouse too much internal opposition.

EXPERTS CANNOT BALANCE COMPETING INTERESTS

A fourth possible argument against government by experts is that experts cannot weigh and balance the competing political claims and interests of different social classes, industries, professions, and regions because this requires experience as a political candidate and leader in a democratic country. The answer to this argument is that the ideal solution to a social problem cannot be determined by balancing the political strength of competing interests. Important social interests often have little or no political power, and when they do have significant power, the amount of this power does not measure the social benefit from satisfying their claims.

Only social scientists can practice felicific calculus, can measure and weigh welfare gains and losses to different persons and groups, and such calculus is always essential to the evaluation of legislative proposals. Politicians can weigh and balance political influence, they can arbitrate and compromise, but only social scientists can measure and compare the social gains and losses from proposed social policies. In other words, rational social welfare calculation differs from rational political calculation and can be practiced only by experts in such calculation, namely applied social scientists.

Felicific calculus is the ideal method of evaluating alternative social policies because nearly all personal and social costs can be measured in a common denominator, money. Because one can buy every obtainable desired social benefit with money, and can avoid every avoidable social real cost by spending money, money can measure all such benefits and costs and make them comparable. The ideal political policy is that which maximizes net social benefit, and felicific calculus is the only method of determining which policy will do this.

Felicific calculation can be applied more easily to economic than to other social problems, and has therefore been more widely discussed and used by welfare economists than by other social scientists, but it is applicable to all political problems. For instance, one can estimate the cost of additional law-enforcement efforts and compare it with the estimated savings from crime reduction.

In a democratic country, voters for and against a proposed law receive, or are supposed to receive, equal attention. But men may vote for a measure because they expect to receive small or large benefits from it, and may vote against it because they expect to receive small or large harm from it. If most affirmative voters properly expect small benefits, and most negative voters great harm, a measure approved by a substantial majority may be socially undesirable. Felicific calculus measures the amount of benefit or harm, and therefore would be preferable to democratic voting even if voters were omniscient.

As noted previously, men do not need the help of social scientists to determine their basic economic and political wants or goals, but they do need such help in combining millions of often conflicting individual wants into rational composite social wants. Government by experts does not require centralized expert choice of social goals. It can and should allow optimum popular influence on the determination of such goals. But specific individual wants and interests conflict. A rational synthesis of private into public interest is therefore necessary, and social scientists can perform this synthesis far more efficiently than democratically elected politicians.

EXPERTS WOULD IMPOSE THEIR CONSUMPTION PATTERNS

Another plausible argument against government by experts is that experts are usually intellectuals or highbrows, with tastes and wants quite different from those of the average man, and would pay far more attention to the wishes of men like themselves than to those of average and inferior men. For instance, they would be inclined to spend too much money on subsidized symphony concerts and too little on subsidized football or baseball games. They might replace too many television westerns with plays by Shaw and Shakespeare. Of course, this evil is an old one. It is common to all governments and organizations run, or strongly influenced by, men of superior ability and education. Thus Protestant ministers in established churches have usually preached sermons well above the intellectual level of their congregations. And state theaters have often favored plays that appeal to sophisticates. Democratic control of such organizations would make their services more pleasing to a larger number of people, but such control would be possible in many organizations—the church, the theater, the concert hall, the publishing industry—under government by experts. For instance, they could be organized and run by independent cooperatives. And in many other organizations—hospitals and clinics, schools and universities—doctors, educators, and other such experts should control the choice of services rendered. Finally, the continued advance of the social sciences will make experts in government ever more aware of the need to please voters and citizens.

GOVERNMENT WORK CAN BE SIMPLIFIED

Another possible argument against government by experts is the claim that government work can be so divided up, simplified, and routinized—for instance, by scientific management and/or bureaucratic organization—that it can be performed by ordinary men without special professional training. Wolin has attributed this idea to Marx and Lenin.[4] It is implicit in some defenses of bureaucracy.

Insofar as this argument is valid, it applies only to subordinate executive functions, not to the function of a nation's chief executive, nor to those of the national legislature. Moreover, even after other higher government functions have been divided up, simplified, and routinized, they still require professional skills. A judge or administrator who handles only patent cases, or even one small class of patent cases, still needs professional training in law and/or in engineering.

I turn now from a discussion of major individual arguments against government by experts to a discussion of other, mostly minor arguments grouped by the name of their proponent. I believe it is worthwhile to review separately the entire case against expert government offered by each of these critics. This will require very little repetition of ideas, itself a very significant fact.

6
The Chief Critics of Government by Experts

I have been discussing the chief possible individual arguments against government by experts. In this chapter, I shall summarize and reply to the case or brief against government by experts or political meritocracy presented by each of the chief critics of these ideas. Because so few critics have explicitly criticized these ideas, I shall also cover the arguments against meritocracy in general that might be used against political meritocracy.

I do not know whether I have been able to discover all of the principal critics of government by experts, but I have not ignored any serious critic I have discovered.

GEORGE SANTAYANA

As noted earlier, George Santayana suggested the idea of government by experts—which he called timocracy—in his *Life of Reason* (1905). He also stated several arguments against it.

First, he asserted (p. 130) that it would be immensely difficult to establish a timocracy because this would require "uprooting the individual from his present natural soil [his environment and family?] and transplanting him to that in which his spirit might flourish best [elite boarding schools?]. It is clear . . . that timocracy would exclude the family or greatly weaken it [by removing children from it or by restricting inheritance?]." He did not explain more precisely what he meant, and I have therefore tried in the bracketed inserts to interpret his claims by means of their context. I believe this argument is largely unsound. Upper-class European and American families have long preferred to send their children to good boarding schools; therefore I do not see why the need for extending this privilege to the most promising children of all classes is a disadvantage of government by experts. Moreover, government by experts would work much better than political democracy even if elite boarding schools were not expanded or multiplied.

Santayana's second argument against timocracy is that it would require "a moral transformation in mankind" because "men must be glad to labour unselfishly. . . . He [the expert] must learn to be happy without wealth, fame, or power . . ." (p. 131). But in fact expert rulers could be as well paid and highly honored as elected politicians now are, if this were desirable. And Santayana admits as much elsewhere: "The competitive motive which socialism is supposed to destroy would be restored in timocracy" (p. 128). By making opportunities more equal, government by experts would encourage the most able men to strive for "wealth, fame, and power." Thus this argument also falls to the ground.

His third argument is that the common people would not benefit materially from expert government, and would therefore have to be motivated by a powerful "patriotism" to accept and endure it (p. 132). But I have given many reasons why expert government would yield substantial material benefits to the great majority of citizens. Santayana does not even try to demonstrate the opposite; he merely asserts it dogmatically.

His fourth argument against government by experts is that because it requires men to be extremely moral, unselfish, and patriotic, it would tend to make men fanatical, and government odious, "for an indoctrinated and collective virtue turns easily to fanaticism; . . . (p. 134). But, as I have explained above, such government does not require unselfish and/or patriotic men.

His final argument is that government by experts would require the elimination of private inheritance, in order to make opportunities more equal, and this would reduce incentives and destroy culture, which is largely aristocratic. It is certainly true that inheritance preserves inequality of opportunity, but much has already been done, and much more will be done, to make opportunities for young people less unequal in democratic countries. Private inheritance will be drastically reduced or eliminated by democratic governments before government by experts is fully achieved. Moreover, government by experts would work better than political democracy even in a society where private inheritance continued.

C. A. R. CROSLAND

As noted earlier, few writers have explicitly criticized government by experts and it is therefore necessary to consider indirect or implicit arguments. Because such a system of government would require much more equalization of opportunities —especially in education and in government service—any argument against such equalization is an indirect or implicit argument against government by experts.

In *The Future of Socialism* (1957), C. A. R. Crosland reviews and criticizes several arguments against equalization of opportunities, and the resulting "competitive ladder" society. First, he noted that some critics—chiefly psychiatrists and anthropologists—claim that such equalization would make men feel even more insecure and discontented because they would fear loss of their positions and prestige to more able competitors (p. 220). This argument is unconvincing to me because it overlooks the fact that although such equalization would make many executives and leaders feel less secure, it would make an equal or greater number of potential replacements feel more confident of promotion. Furthermore, it would stimulate both current leaders and their potential successors to study and work harder. Competition between persons always increases personal efforts and achievements. That is why the great majority of economists have endorsed such competition.

The advantages of competition are so obvious and important that supporters of capitalism have long argued that capitalism is superior to socialism chiefly because it favors competition. But in fact a socialist state could and should notably increase competition between persons (not between firms) by making opportunities much more equal. And a recognition of this truth is implicit in the above argument against equalization of opportunities. It is paradoxical that in one case some supporters of the present order should argue against such equalization, and in the other case for it.

Socialism would, of course, greatly increase economic security for all by ending business fluctuations and unemployment, and by insuring all men against nearly all risks. Thus men might feel more secure in spite of the increase in competition for personal advancement. Those who failed in this competition would suffer much less economic hardship than failures now suffer under capitalism. And socialism will be largely achieved before government by experts.

Crosland also reports that some critics allege that equalization of opportunities will increase and intensify the sense of failure:

> A hereditary society, denying the opportunity to rise, avoids also the sense of failure at not having risen, but if all have the opportunity, and only 10 percent succeed, 90 percent are conscious of having failed, and suffer a loss of self-esteem (p. 220).

But we already have a competitive system under which most men fail to rise as high as they wish, and the achievement of equal opportunity under government by experts would not increase the percentage of failure. It would merely assure that those who rise deserve to rise. Those who fail solely because of equalization of opportunities would be replaced by an equal number of men who would rise as a result of the new system. Moreover, the new successes would enjoy their success more fully because they would have more reason to believe in their own merit. And the men they replace might feel their failure less keenly because they would know it to be both deserved and socially beneficial.

When men who deserve to succeed fail to do so, and see less competent men rise above them, they feel frustration and/or bitterness as well as a sense of failure. Moreover, they know their failure reduces national income and welfare. When men fail to succeed because of equalization of opportunities, they become aware that their failure is a result of their heredity and past experience, not of discrimination or inefficient methods of promotion. They therefore feel less frustration and less resentment than would more able men who deserved to succeed.

Another possible but unsound charge against any system that would make opportunities more equal, according to Crosland, is that it would make men more acquisitive "inasmuch as higher status depends, in Veblenesque fashion, on high consumption standards, and so on making money" (p. 220). But if acquisitive men could acquire wealth and income only by benefiting society to an equal or greater degree, any measure that makes men more acquisitive would be socially desirable. And if men are still free to acquire wealth by means that harm society, we should rule out the use of such means, not measures that make men acquisitive.

Although he rejects these three arguments against meritocracy, Crosland states with apparent approval what he calls "the fundamental ethical case against any elite," namely that selection of an elite must be based on certain "measurable aspects of character," which are not the only ones ethically relevant. "Why should no marks be given for saintliness, generosity, compassion, humor, beauty, assiduity, continence, or artistic ability?" he asks (p. 236). One answer is that if these traits are unmeasurable, we cannot know they affect the individual productivity of rulers. The claim that they are ethically relevant, like all ethical theories, is literally senseless because it is impossible to think of any way to verify it. What practical difference does it make whether leaders are selected ethically or unethically? All that is needed is to select them so as to maximize agreed indices of measurable efficiency, and Crosland admits that unethical selection would do this.

I do not think that Crosland really objects to entrusting the functions of government to those most competent to perform them. I suspect that what he dislikes is the idea of rewarding such experts more highly than other men, or than many equally talented men in other fields. But, of course, such rewards for government experts would not be necessary under government by experts. There is no good reason why political leaders should be paid more than the best artists, doctors, scientists, or preachers. And in fact in democratic states they are not the best paid men.

PEREGRINE WORSTHORNE

Government by experts would be political meritocracy. Perhaps the most comprehensive statement of the case against all meritocracy is that offered by Peregrine Worsthorne in an article in *Encounter* (London) in 1956.[1] This article, "The New Inequality, More Dangerous than the Old," is a defense of the British ruling class, largely aristocratic or plutocratic, against the rising meritocracy. Unlike most earlier ruling-class theorists, Worsthorne does not waste any time trying to prove that every past society has had, and every future society will have, a small ruling class or political elite. Instead he takes this for granted and begins by calling attention to the rapid contemporary transfer of business and political power from one elite, those who inherit titles and/or wealth, to another, those who have received professional training and have earned high position by merit. He fears that this trend will continue until no one inherits business or political power, and he offers several reasons why we should strive to prevent this result.

His first reason is that meritocrats will make fewer mistakes. "The exercise of power," he claims, " . . . is far too comprehensive, far too easy, far too irresistible to be left to professional elites whose authority is undiluted by the habitual weaknesses and failings of a hereditary ruling class" (p. 28). On another page, he explains that the Russian Revolution was attributable to the failings of the hereditary Russian ruling class, but it is clear that he is not referring to such failings in the above quotation. He has a higher opinion of the British establishment, which is less exclusive. But he does fear that a British political meritocracy would be too efficient, probably for the same reasons that many authors of the American Constitution feared that a strong democratic federal government would be too efficient and progressive. In America, the division and limitation of government powers perform the same function, the slowing down of progress, that Worsthorne believes is performed by the Establishment in Britain. Like Washington, Adams, and Hamilton, Worsthorne is a conservative who fears that democratic egalitarian trends will steadily reduce the unearned special privileges of his social caste.

His second reason for opposing complete political meritocracy is that, "resistance to power today can only be effective in a society where the lower strata contain men of independence and ability who would have been creamed off at birth [in a meritocracy]" (p. 28). In other words, we must reject and discriminate against some superior men so that they can lead the lower strata in their protests against the unsound policies of the government, one which he had previously claimed is preferable because it would make more mistakes. But would it not be better to select able men and appoint them as well-paid agents or leaders of the lower strata? We now have paid public defenders, ombudsmen, union leaders, personnel experts, and social workers to defend and/or lead these strata, and their numbers, authority, and ability could be greatly increased in a meritocracy. I can see no need deliberately to create frustrated, maladjusted spokesmen for the unfortunate, nor any reason why there should be any substantial numbers of economic unfortunates in a socialist meritocracy.

Worsthorne's third argument is that in a meritocracy "promotion . . . will depend *entirely* [his italics] on a man's ability and willingness to conform." Worsthorne is wise enough to realize that insistence on conformity is socially undesirable, but he assumes without explanation that the highly intelligent and educated leaders of a meritocracy would not know as much! Furthermore, his argument implies that politicians now have little need to conform to public opinion in order to be elected. He seems unaware that our age has often been called the age of conformity. I believe that the able social scientists and administrators of a meritocracy would do much more to encourage and reward constructive new ideas than do contemporary voters and politicians.

The rise of government by experts will mean the end of political democracy, but not of freedom of press and speech, as is sometimes claimed. Social scientists support freedom of press and speech more fervently than do any other class of citizens because they are scientists and because as social scientists they have suffered more from censorship than any other class of scientists. All men of science know that freedom of press and speech favors the growth of science, and all classes of scientists have suffered from censorship and persecution, but during the last century or two social scientists have suffered much more than other scientists. We may therefore be confident that a government of social scientists would support freedom of press and speech more earnestly than has any democratic government.

Like a variety of other writers, Worsthorne stresses the fact that members of an hereditary aristocracy or plutocracy are economically independent and can therefore criticize government policies without fear of economic coercion. But modern states often imprison, blacklist, or otherwise discriminate against unorthodox rich men for their political opinions. And unemployment and ostracism are fearful penalties, even for wealthy men, for instance, wealthy scientists, movie stars, and script writers. Thus, very few men of wealth now go out of their way to defend unpopular causes or blacklisted individuals. Hitler found it easy to coerce or ruin men of wealth and/or noble birth.

Worsthorne's fourth reason for rejecting meritocracy is that an elite that does not include many "foolish," "inept," and "useless" members could not understand the common people. It would be "cut off . . . from the rest of society that had not made the grade" (p. 29). Here again he assumes he is much wiser than the elite of a political meritocracy could be. They could easily hire "foolish, inept, and useless" informants and consultants if they were needed. But it is highly unlikely they would be needed. His reasoning implies that able psychiatrists cannot

The Chief Critics of Government by Experts

help their patients as much as foolish ones or that able teachers cannot teach as well as inept ones. Finally, we do not need an hereditary ruling class to supply us with a set of rulers who include some ordinary or inferior men. We could easily achieve this result by choosing some leaders by lot, as the ancient Greeks did.

Worsthorne's fifth reason is that society would be "more rigid and unfraternal" "if those at the top not only felt but *were* superior and those at the bottom not only felt but were inferior—and knew it." (p. 29). Of course, this result could be achieved only if all men were free to rise, and did so, according to their ability. Such a society is obviously not "rigid." And it is equally absurd to imply that frustration of some able men would make them feel more fraternal, or would be justifiable even if it did.

It is noteworthy that many defenders of aristocracy and oligarchy have argued that aristocrats and oligarchs are superior men. Worsthorne is the first to argue that they should rule because some of them are inferior. He can at least claim the merit of originality!

His sixth reason is more conventional, namely that leaders selected for merit will try to pass on their privileges to their children, and thus create an hereditary ruling class. Of course, this would produce all the benefits he has previously attributed to rule by such a class, but he fails to note this embarrassing fact. Instead, he criticizes at length and rejects several methods proposed by egalitarians to prevent meritocracy from degenerating into rule by an hereditary upper class.

If the experts who rule a meritocracy are not paid much more than the average worker, they will have no incentive to perform well, according to Wortsthorne, and if financial inducements sufficient to induce good performance are paid, these experts will be able to give their children very superior advantages and thus create an hereditary ruling class. This argument is unsound for a variety of reasons.

It is piece rates and other intra-occupational incentives, not inter-occupational income differentials, that persuade individuals to increase individual output, but such incentives do not create social classes. Such classes are created by inter-occupational wage and salary differentials, which are largely the result of monopoly and/or special privilege. Thus it would be easy to reduce the average wages of physicians to those of carpenters, by increasing the number of doctors, without reducing the incentive of doctors to earn more money by treating more patients. Indeed, such a reduction of average incomes would probably increase the incentive effects of our piecework medical-fee system.

The coming egalitarian society will increase opportunities for all kinds of professional education, and will expand total social investment in such education until the average net earnings of each profession have fallen close to the national average of all workers. Gross earnings will exceed net earnings enough to amortize the costs of professional education, but the difference will go directly or indirectly to professional schools. Professional work is more interesting and more respected than most other work; therefore no incentive will be needed to attract men to such work when their professional education is free or is adequately financed by loans repaid out of excess earnings.

MICHAEL YOUNG

Because no serious scholarly book on meritocracy has appeared, *The Rise of Meritocracy, 1870-2033* (1958), a satirical novel by Michael Young, is perhaps the most important book on this subject. In Chapter 2, I reviewed Young's reasons for the rise of meritocracy. Here I shall discuss his principal arguments against meritocracy. I shall ignore such minor, dubious points as his suggestion that amorous upper-class women might prefer athletic dullards to less muscular geniuses. All of these arguments, both serious and trivial, are attributed by Young to conservative and populist rebels of the year 2033 against meritocracy, but they seem to be his own. And most critics of the book have taken many of these arguments seriously.

First, the author repeats the claim that after meritocracy is firmly established, the meritocrats will seek to make high offices hereditary. The practice of meritocracy, which requires equalization of educational opportunities, will soon segregate superior genes in a small hereditary elite, which will then demand a special superior education for its children and grandchildren. He even describes this as having happened before the year 2033 (pp. 141-42).

It is true, of course, that meritocracy will tend to segregate superior genes in the upper class, but, in the absence of radical eugenic measures—and he suggests none—this process will require many centuries. Moreover, meritocrats, like all previous rulers, will have to earn and maintain popular support, which would be endangered by the rise of hereditary power. Indeed, Young describes a rebellion before the year 2033 in part caused by this development. He assumes that meritocrats (I.Q. over 160) would not be bright enough to recognize and avoid this danger.

Moreover, because the children of meritocrats would, on average, be very superior—though not as superior as their parents—they would do well even without any special hereditary privileges. Thus their parents would feel little need to give them such privileges.

Furthermore, because meritocrats would be very able and highly educated people, they would be more socially minded and much more eager for social progress than average men. They would also be well aware of the harmful effects of hereditary privilege. For both reasons they would be less tempted than any previous elite to try to make their positions or power hereditary.

Finally, the chief advantage of hereditary wealth or power is that it yields an income far above the average. If differences in personal income are radically reduced before government by experts is adopted—as I predict they will be—the temptation to make political leadership hereditary will be further reduced.

Young's second major point against meritocracy is that inequality is unpopular and immoral. Men will "oppose inequality because it reflects a narrowness of values. They deny that one man is in any fundamental way the superior of another. They seek the equality of man in the sense that they want every man to be respected for the good that is in him. Every man is a genius at something, . . ." (p. 135).

This is a curious mixture of nonsense and error. The "values" referred to are presumably moral or ethical, and therefore senseless, like all moral propositions. The claim that no one is superior "in any fundamental way" is likewise senseless because it is impossible to conceive of any way of disproving it. The phrase "in any fundamental way" is a metaphysical, not a scientific, term. And the assertion that "every man is a genius at something" is obviously and demonstratably false, unless the term "genius" is defined so as to make the proposition unverifiable and meaningless.

The idea that every man should be "respected for the good that is in him" is senseless because it contains two terms, "should" and "good," which, here, are moral rather than scientific terms. No statement containing either term can be verified by scientific observation unless these terms are defined so as to make this possible, and Young does not offer, refer to, or even imply the possibility of such definitions.

It is possible, of course, to offer scientific arguments against inequality of average incomes between different regions, industries, or professions; or against inequality of power between different men or groups of men. But Young does not interpret his criticism of inequality as a criticism of any such specific and testable policy.

Moreover, neither government by experts nor meritocracy requires that personal incomes be more or less unequal than under democracy or dictatorship. I have argued elsewhere that in an ideal society personal incomes should be far less unequal than they now are, but my argument is as valid in a democratic society as in one ruled by experts.

On the other hand, every society must be organized, must have leaders and subordinates, if it is to function efficiently and maximize social welfare. The resulting inequality in power—there need be no great inequality in income—is socially desirable because it benefits all men in many ways. If Young means to imply that such inequality is undesirable he is clearly in error.

In further developing his questionable argument against inequality, Young asserts that the ideal "classless society would be one which both possessed and acted upon plural [ethical?] values. Were we to evaluate people, not only according to their intelligence and their education, their occupation and their power, but according to their kindliness and their courage, their sympathy and generosity, there could be no classes" (p. 135).

Here Young is confusing personal evaluation of character with evaluation of economic productivity or managerial ability. Meritocracy and government by experts need not change or determine personal respects and evaluation of character. They only require the gradations of authority essential for efficient social production and consumption. They do not require us to pay leaders more than subordinates, or to evaluate leaders as morally superior to subordinates.

It would be very foolish to choose business or political leaders "according to their kindliness and their courage, their sympathy and generosity." Such leaders should be chosen entirely on the basis of their professional training and record of success. We may deeply respect kindly, courageous, sympathetic, generous housewives and factory workers, but such respect would not justify their choice as legislators or government officials.

Government by experts is desirable and inevitable because it will result in a very beneficial division of labor. It will assign the functions of government to those who, by training and experience, are best qualified to perform them. But a division of labor does not itself necessarily create social classes. It is wide income differentials, not wide occupational differences, that create and perpetuate social classes. Income differentials can and will be radically reduced, even while the division of labor is becoming ever more intensive.

Like Crosland, Young argues that inferior men cannot stand the psychological burden of having their inferiority exposed by reliable meritocratic tests and evaluations (pp. 86-87). But he predicts that under meritocracy all men will be paid the same wages (p. 127); so it is therefore hard to understand why they would strongly resent the results of such tests. In any case, most men are now tested and evaluated. Furthermore, the scientific point of view, which is steadily spreading, is that success in life is entirely determined by heredity and environment, so that no one should be much praised for great success or much blamed for great failure. Finally, if everyone is a genius, or even competent, at something, everyone should have cause for some unjustified pride.

The great social tragedy, of course, is that some men are born defective and/or are raised in a bad environment and are then punished all of their lives for this great misfortune. Children born crippled, blind, or feeble-minded are heavily penalized all their lives because they live in a calloused society. The mere measurement and exposure of these and lesser handicaps would not place an undue psychological burden on the less fortunate. Rather it would be part of a testing system that would permit the selection of more able leaders, who would certainly reduce the personal economic penalties of such handicaps.

Young restates Worsthorne's argument that the growing practice of meritocracy will drain the English lower classes of nearly all superior intelligence. He suggests this may occur within two or three generations (pp. 11-12). Yet critics of proposed eugenic reforms have long argued that it would take hundreds of years to achieve a small part of this result. The lower-class gene pool is so large and so mixed that it can continue to yield some superior progeny for many generations, in spite of any drain due to meritocracy. Furthermore, the bad effects of any segregation of inferior genes can and will be offset by eugenic measures—such as sterilizing the least fit—before government by experts is fully achieved.

Even if the lower classes do not lose potential political leaders before birth as a result of gene segregation, they will lose them after birth as a result of the democratization of education and political meritocracy. The gifted children of the working classes will all secure university degrees and become professionals and executives. Young suggests that this will injure the working classes because no one can understand their problems unless he himself is a worker (pp. 132-33). He implies that sound

The Chief Critics of Government by Experts

political decision-making requires the participation of men with long work-experience in each important occupation. This is an unsound theory. It ignores the great advantages of specialized professional education and experience and of the division of labor. These advantages were explained in detail in Chapter 3, and need not be repeated here.

Young discusses at some length the effect of future mechanization and automation on employment. He suggests that by 1988 one third of the British labor force will be "unemployable in the ordinary economy . . . due to lack of intelligence" (p. 96). Thus, some ten million of these unemployable will be employed as domestic servants (p. 98). The resulting increase in servile employment will re-create or strengthen class lines.

These predictions are completely unsound. Mechanization has been going on for over two hundred years in Great Britain without causing any increase in unemployment, and it need not increase unemployment in the future. Economic wants as a whole are insatiable. Moreover, as personal incomes become less unequal, the proportion of people who can afford to hire full or part-time servants will decline steadily. And domestic labor-saving devices will continue to grow in number and efficiency. Thus the proportion of domestic servants in the British population will certainly continue to decline indefinitely.

I have criticized this reasoning on employment because it is set forth in Young's discussion of the rise and fall of meritocracy, which implies that it is relevant to this rise and fall. In fact, I feel it is quite irrelevant. If mechanization and automation produce a growing unemployment, they will tend to do so under any form of government. There is no plausible reason to believe that the rise of government by experts will increase technological unemployment. Indeed, experts ought to be more successful than anyone else in minimizing this or any other undesired social consequence.

One other irrelevant reason given by Young for his predicted rebellion against meritocracy deserves note. In describing the rise of meritocracy he ably explains the advantages to be gained from segregating very superior children in separate educational channels or schools and predicts that such segregation will grow as meritocracy develops. However, he expects that the parents of other children will object to this segregation and that some of them will rebel against the meritocratic government of 2033, in part for this reason.

This prediction is illogical because segregation of superior students is not necessary under meritocracy. Like many other possible reforms, it would make meritocracy, or any other form of government, more efficient, but meritocracy could function well with or without it.

Incidentally, Young asserts that the segregation of students by ability would mean the abandonment of "equality of opportunity" (p. 144). But if it resulted in better education for all classes—through the use of texts and educational methods better suited to the abilities of each class of students—it would give all students better opportunities to succeed in life. The term "equality of educational opportunity" does not imply that all students must have the same education or be taught in the same classes. It implies that each student should be able to go as far as his ability permits him to go, and segregation of students by interest and ability favors the achievement of this goal.

Finally, the chief reason parents now object to segregation of students by ability is that they fear this will reduce the subsequent earnings of their children. The coming radical reduction in inter-occupational income differentials will greatly weaken this ground for objection to such segregation.

BERNARD CRICK

In his book *In Defense of Politics* (1962), Bernard Crick defines politics as "the activity by which differing interests within a given territory are conciliated" (p. 167). Political democracy is a form of politics and, according to Crick, government by experts is not (pp. 20-21); thus his defense of politics is also a defense of democratic government against expert government.

His defense is at times clever and at other times obscure. For instance, he emphasizes that both Communists and Nazis

The Chief Critics of Government by Experts

claim to be scientific, and implies that social theorists who claim to be scientific therefore resemble these unpopular ideologists (pp. 98-101). It is true, of course, that Marx was a pioneer in social science, but Hitler was certainly not a scientist or an admirer of science. He was born a Catholic and never left the church or rejected religious thinking. In his last months he repeatedly asked for divine aid on the German radio network.

Crick believes that politics, preferably democratic politics, is badly needed because it alone can determine and reconcile conflicting social interest. "The political system deals in priorities" among interest or values. Government by experts is not a political system because "there is a single authoritative source for the allocation of values and for the determination of policies" (p. 171).

The implication is that economic interests—like an industry's request for a higher tariff—or religious prejudices—like opposition to abortion—can be better determined and weighed by politicians than by social scientists, but Crick does not attempt to prove this, he merely asserts or implies it repeatedly. For instance, his frequent use of the terms "value" and "ethical commitment" implies that values are supernatural or philosophical and should not be questioned by social scientists. And he is unwilling to admit that scientists are more objective and more competent to evaluate arguments for tariffs and abortion control than are politicians.

In the previous chapter I explained why social policy determinations should be based on felicific calculus, not on the political balancing of conflicting interests. Crick seems completely unaware of the nature and advantages of felicific calculation. He does not try to explain why political bargaining is superior to rational economic calculation. He probably considers such calculation immoral, at least when it questions traditional moral prejudices.

The claim of social scientists that they alone can solve social problems and prescribe the best social policies is called "scientism" by Crick. He refers to Lasswell's belief that social scientists can reduce or prevent social tension and conflict, and asserts dogmatically that "such a politics of prevention is not politics . . . and it is not science" because "genuine understanding, true scholarship, pure science . . . inevitably involves political values." This argument is typically vague and unconvincing, but it illustrates his anti-scientific bias.

Crick implies that scientists cannot deal with "political values." However, as noted earlier, most such values do not concern ultimate ends, but are mere economic interests or unjustified prejudices concerning methods of operation or management. For instance, independent store operators desire or value special taxes on chain stores, while chain-store operators want or value freedom from such taxes. And ultimate values, such as the desire for more food, clothing and housing, are as obvious to scientists as to moralists and politicians.

After indicting social scientists for their inability to understand and use political values—which are personal prejudices or wants—Crick proceeds to accuse them of being subject to human emotions. He asserts that the social scientists "will not succeed in becoming passionless" and so cannot be free from prejudice. His theories are therefore "doctrines," like religious dogmas, not objective scientific generalizations (pp. 101-2). The unstated implication is that social science is as questionable as popular political prejudice.

This is but one of many evidences that Crick is anti-intellectual and anti-scientific. Although he does not explain his personal point of view, his repeated attacks on science suggest that he is fundamentally religious or philosophic. He repeatedly implies that there are valid unscientific methods of discovering factual principles and/or determining sound social policies, but he does not explain or illustrate the use of any such method, except by his own fallacious reasoning.

Crick argues that politics maximizes freedom and that the elimination of politics would seriously reduce freedom (pp. 186-88). This is obviously true of freedom to vote, but not of other freedoms. If voters surrender their freedom to vote on complicated social issues and entrust the solution of social problems to experts, the experts might, and I believe would, solve these

The Chief Critics of Government by Experts

problems in such a way as to increase personal freedom. For instance, they would speed up the rise in real wages, and every rise in personal real income makes men free to do things they could not have done before.

When a man goes to a doctor for medical treatment, he gives up his freedom to treat himself because he has confidence in his doctor. And the resulting improvement in his health expands his overall freedom by enabling him to do things he could not otherwise have done. If social scientists know more than laymen about social problems, voters who give up their freedom to vote and entrust the solution of their problems to social scientists increase their personal freedom just as they do when they entrust their medical problems to doctors.

It is noteworthy that although Crick and Young are both members of the small English academic community, Crick ignored the arguments for and against political meritocracy stated in Young's *The Rise of Meritocracy*, which appeared four years before Crick published his book and which attracted considerable attention. It is also significant that Young did not bother to discuss the chief arguments against non-political government used later by Crick, arguments which are not new.

DAVID RIESMAN

David Riesman, the well-known American sociologist, has also recently published a criticism of meritocracy. He begins by restating a religious argument against all meritocracy:

> The scientific and rationalist temper of . . . meritocracy may undermine . . . morale . . . it has no religious base. Is America's romance with practicality and efficiency enough to sustain it? Men serving a system with no goal other than its own further advance have no transcendent aims. [One can criticize them for] sustaining a self-perpetuating structure, rather than helping to cure the diseases of society.[2]

The first point, that meritocracy needs a religious base and/or transcendent aims, is mere religious dogma. The steady improvement in personal and social behavior during the past few centuries has been accompanied by an almost continuous decline in religious faith in advanced countries. Both trends are likely to continue indefinitely, and are probably causally related. Social reformers have long been less religious than social conservatives.

There is, of course, a fundamental conflict between religion and science, especially social science. Religious men believe that personal, and therefore social decisions and acts are free, unpredictable acts, i.e., not determined by heredity and environment. Scientists assume that all such decisions and acts are so determined. Religious men believe that the chief purpose of all people and all societies should be to please some god or gods. Scientists believe that men seek only to achieve personal happiness, contentment, satisfaction, or well-being, and that governments do or should try to maximize social welfare, the sum of such desired personal well-being.

A government by experts in government selected by social scientists would be a government by scientists. This explains much of the opposition to such government, even by men who call themselves scientists. Many scientists are scientific only when dealing with certain kinds of problems, those within their specialty, and are religious in their thinking about many other problems.

Most religious people, including many scientists, still believe that governments should enforce certain religious and moral rules—on Sunday rest, religious oaths, abortion, birth control, divorce, homosexual behavior, and so on. It is very unlikely that a government of experts would continue indefinitely to use the police and courts to enforce such controversial religious and moral dogmas. Thus, religious men will long continue to oppose government by experts.

However, as noted earlier, the influence of religion has been declining for centuries, and will certainly continue to decline indefinitely. Furthermore, a government of competent social scientists would be aware of all popular religious prejudices and would be careful not to offend religious people enough to cause undue violence.

Riesman calls meritocracy "a system with no goal other than

its own further advance." But a system cannot have goals. And there is no reason whatever to believe that the men who create, support, and/or staff a meritocracy would be interested *only* in the advance of meritocracy. Are the men who support democratic government interested *only* in the advance of democracy? It seems obvious to me that nearly all men have many goals other than the advance of some political system. And, of all men, scientists are the most likely to treat social institutions as means to ends rather than as ends in themselves.

The closely related assertion that meritocrats would strive merely to "sustain a self-perpetuating structure" rather than "to cure the disease of society" is equally dogmatic and unsound. There is every reason to expect that meritocrats would be more eager to solve social problems, and much more efficient in solving them, than aristocrats or democratic politicians. Able men enjoy solving problems and doing so efficiently. The chief obstacles to social reform have always been vested economic interests, ignorance, and incompetence. As explained previously, meritocrats would be much less hampered by these obstacles than previous rulers.

Riesman also raises the question of whether it is possible to select the most intelligent and able men:

> One of the problems [of meritocracy] . . . is the nature of the formal tests for achievement. . . . These are universalistic . . . But many people believe that such tests do not take into account the more impalpable or less easily measurable personal qualities.[3]

This criticism applies of course to all use of formal tests of education and achievement. It implies that all civil service systems are imperfect because formal tests cannot measure certain qualities. It is true that no system of measuring education and ability will ever be perfect, but this is a very weak argument against the use of the best available systems. The desired qualities that cannot be measured by formal tests probably cannot be measured by personal observation.

Moreover, if personal opinion of candidates for high office is a useful supplement to formal tests in evaluating candidates for high public office, such opinion can be used in an undemocratic as well as in a democratic government. Indeed, by relying only on the opinion of a wisely selected few, we should be able to do much better than by relying on the personal opinions of all adults as voters.

Everyone who does badly on a formal test is tempted to excuse himself by criticizing the test. Thus, however efficient such tests become, some of those who fail to do well in them will criticize the tests used. But such biased criticism will always be suspect.

Finally, Riesman fears that "where meritocracy is unidimensional and based on measured intelligence and skill, there may be a tendency for manners to decline and for people to become less receptive to charm."[4] But because good manners and charm make executives more efficient, tests of executive achievement should certainly measure the results of manners and charm, as well as those of other desired executive traits. Of course, manners and charm are relatively unproductive in some occupations, like scientific research, but this means that we do not need to measure them in testing men for these occupations. The important point is that all traits that are productive can be measured indirectly as a group by measuring the product, and no other traits need to be measured.

Riesman's arguments against meritocracy are notably weak and fanciful. The fact that a celebrated social scientist takes such arguments seriously is itself a stronger argument against government by social scientists than any advanced by Riesman. However, social science will make great advances during the next two hundred years.

T. D. WELDON

The Vocabulary of Politics (1953) by T. D. Weldon, an English philosopher, is primarily devoted to an able exposure of the widespread use of meaningless, pre-scientific words in traditional political philosophy, but it contains some comments on government by experts which deserve criticism here.

The Chief Critics of Government by Experts

In a section entitled "Philosopher Kings," Weldon argues that the idea of government by experts is unsound because there is no separate science of government in which experts may specialize. Wise rulers should have a general, not a specialized education. They should employ and rely on experts of many kinds, but should not themselves be experts (pp. 138-40).

There is some truth implicit in this very plausible argument. Rulers should not be narrow experts, but, on the other hand, they should not be complete generalists. For instance, a legislator does not need to know as much about astronomy, mathematics, chemistry, physics, geology, medicine, law, art, military strategy, and many other subjects as he needs to know about economics, political science, and sociology. Expert rulers should have professional training in one or more social sciences, but they should not be narrow specialists in any special field, even of social science.

Weldon's argument that there is no special science of ruling for rulers to study applies with equal logic to business administration. Business managers can and do make wide use of experts and deal with a wide variety of problems, but this does not mean that they cannot benefit from graduate, professional training in business administration. The keen demand for graduates with such training proves that practical business executives place a high value on it.

Weldon claims that "government by experts is not usually good government just because experts tend to be obsessed by their own expertise and to ignore points of view which differ from their own" (p. 139). If valid, this argument would seem to apply with equal force to business executives with professional training in business administration. But students in both business and public administration can be, and are, taught to respect the views of other experts and of the public. And the more intelligent and successful the administrator or social scientist, the more likely he is to give adequate consideration to relevant points of view different from his own. Indeed, this should be a significant advantage of government by the most able experts.

Weldon asserts that rulers have only one major function, to

"exercise authority and make decisions" (p. 141), and implies that this cannot be taught. He ignores the vital fact that one can make decisions much more wisely after one has studied the problems with which one is dealing, and that nearly all problems faced by rulers belong to the social sciences. Moreover, American professional schools of business administration, public administration, military science, and other subjects have long been teaching their students how to make high-level decisions.

FINAL COMMENTS

Now that I have completed my review of the arguments against meritocracy in general and political meritocracy in particular, I wish to comment on the general impression they make.

First, it is remarkable how many different arguments have been stated. Some thirty points have been presented and criticized above.

Second, it is notable that they cover a wide range of ideas and differ from each other to a surprising extent.

Third, there is much less duplication of arguments among the various individual critics than one would expect. Each critic offers a largely unique case against political meritocracy. And few quote other critics. This suggests both that these critics are unfamiliar with most of the scant literature on the subject and that they have little respect for the literature and arguments they are familiar with. They have certainly been unable to agree among themselves as to which arguments are the most important, and even as to which are sound.

Fourth, most of the arguments appear illogical, irrelevant, or fanciful. This may explain why so few critics have noted or repeated the arguments used by other critics. It suggests that they have devoted very little time and thought to the ideas they are criticizing. One gets the impression that nearly all of them are merely summarizing their first superficial reaction to distasteful proposals. I predict that further study will lead to the radical revision or abandonment of nearly all of these tentative arguments.

The most frequently stated or implied argument is the idea that social policy determination should be based on ethical principles. This is a relapse into pre-scientific or anti-scientific thinking. It reminds us that religious and philosophic beliefs are still the chief obstacles to scientific thinking about human behavior. Many modern writers have not yet accepted Comte's claim that social as well as natural phenomena can and should be studied in an objective, unbiased, scientific manner.

This old and still influential ethical argument against the scientific determination of social policies deserves much more space than I have given it. But I have written a book, *Religion, Philosophy, and Science*, largely devoted to this subject and I do not wish to repeat more of it here.

7

The Transition to Government by Experts

In this chapter I shall predict the way in which government by experts will be achieved, both in democratic and undemocratic countries. In other words, I shall describe the coming transition from democracy and dictatorship to government by experts in government. Because I live in a democratic state and am writing chiefly for readers in such states, and because social change is more orderly and predictable in these states, I shall devote most of my discussion to the transition in advanced democratic states. One major purpose of my discussion of this transition is to clarify and illustrate my prediction of the rise of government by experts. Another purpose is to make this prediction more plausible.

THE TRANSITION IN DEMOCRATIC STATES

Every new social or political system begins and grows for a long time within the old. In democratic states the transition to government by experts has been under way for many years and will continue for many more before the new system becomes predominant. This change has been and will continue to be largely peaceful. There will be no violent overthrow of the old system by supporters of the new, at least not in mature democracies.

The transition may be hastened or delayed by one or more nuclear wars and/or by a prolongation and intensification of the cold war. I shall ignore such influences because they and their effects will be temporary and are especially hard to predict. In

The Transition to Government by Experts

other words, I shall confine my discussion to normal, peace-time social trends. These are much easier to predict than individual historical events.

I explained in Chapter 3 why most major long-run general social trends are steadily making government by experts more necessary and more politically feasible. In this chapter I shall explain how certain minor and less general trends are increasing the participation and influence of experts in government.

I shall begin by discussing social trends that are relatively old and/or well established.

Old Trends Leading to Government by Experts
THE GROWTH OF CIVIL SERVICE

The steady growth of the civil service system, which implies the decline of the spoils system, of choosing government employees, especially executives and professionals, is a significant trend toward government by experts. This trend will continue in all advanced countries until all subordinate executives and professionals are civil service appointees. Because higher civil servants are usually experts, the growth of civil service will amount to a trend toward expert government.

Moreover, the methods of selecting and promoting civil servants will be continuously improved. And of course the proportion of the national labor force employed by the government will rise for centuries. As a result, the demand for professionally trained experts in government will grow, and this in turn will stimulate efforts to develop the social sciences and to provide an ever larger number of better educated experts in government. Thus, by the time government by experts is fully achieved, the supply of able and experienced government experts will be far larger than it now is, relatively as well as absolutely. And voters and legislators will become ever more accustomed to relying on the services of experts in government.

THE GROWING EMPLOYMENT OF CITY AND COUNTY MANAGERS

Until seventy years ago, all American city and county governments were managed by elected officials—mayors, directors, supervisors. In the first decade of this century, civic reformers began to advocate the replacement of the mayor-council system of city government by the city-manager system. Under the latter system, the routine management of city government is entrusted to a professionally trained city manager who devotes his life to such work, usually beginning as an assistant to a city manager in a small city and, if successful, being appointed to a similar or higher rank in larger and larger cities.

The city-manager system has also been adopted by some counties. It has proven itself to be increasingly successful and popular in the United States, and has spread to Canada and Ireland. By 1968 over two thousand cities and counties in the United States were managed by city or county managers instead of elected officials. This trend will continue indefinitely. By 2100 nearly all cities and counties in English-speaking countries will be managed by professional city managers with higher university degrees in public administration. Moreover, they will suffer less and less from interference and pressure by elected city councilmen and county supervisors. Their pay, prestige, and freedom will increase steadily as men become more and more aware of the benefits of expert government.

MORE AUTONOMY FOR GOVERNMENT AGENCIES

More and more government agencies will be partially freed from political control by national legislatures and executives and set up as semi-independent agencies managed by competent experts. This trend will be most obvious in the case of government-owned public utilities and business enterprises, but it will also affect public universities, research agencies, and regulatory commissions. In this process, the enactment of laws by democratically elected legislators will be increasingly replaced by the formulation of administrative rulings by appointed experts employed by semi-autonomous public agencies.

The Transition to Government by Experts

For instance, the United States Post Office Department has just been separated from the federal administrative bureaucracy and set up as a semi-independent government corporation. It is now authorized to choose its own nonpolitical, professional executives, to determine their salaries, to fix and alter all postal rates, to establish operating policies, to make all investment decisions, to sell bonds, and to select the location of new post offices. Most other advanced nations will soon follow this example.

Socialists have long stressed the fact that the management of large private corporations is now highly undemocratic and have argued that it should and will become more democratic. But in fact the management of these corporations is now more efficient than that of most large government agencies precisely because private managers are more likely to be experts and/or to be free from detailed control by politicians. Now that the United States Post Office has been turned into a corporation, it will become much more efficient because it will be freed from most control by Congress and from its non-expert politician administrators. The TVA is much more efficient than the old Post Office system because it resembles a private corporation more than a department of government. Thus the thesis of this book implies that governments will become more like private corporations, which conflicts with the oft-heard socialist claim that private corporations will become more democratic under socialism.

During the next fifty years almost every advanced capitalist nation will create a semi-independent economic-stabilization agency authorized to raise and lower certain income or sales taxes and some forms of widely and immediately felt public spending—such as old-age pensions—in order to achieve and maintain full employment. These stabilization agencies will be run by economists and will be increasingly freed from political influence.

Because the achievement and maintenance of near full employment under capitalism will cause undue inflation as long as businessmen are free to raise their prices whenever they wish, all advanced capitalist countries will establish national price-control agencies during the next few decades. And these new agencies will gradually become autonomous bureaus run by economists because political control of individual prices, or those who control them, is very undesirable.

The function of determining the wages, hours of labor, and working conditions of federal civil servants, now performed by the Congress, will soon be delegated to personnel experts in the United States Civil Service Commission or in the employing agencies. The same thing will happen in state and local government.

Many other old and new government agencies manned by civil servants who are professional experts will be authorized to perform more and more functions now performed by democratically elected legislatures and local councils.

In the United States a wide variety of powerful autonomous federal agencies—such as the Atomic Energy Commission and the Federal Trade Commission—have already been created, but most of them are still controlled by political appointees. Some of the major independent agencies created to regulate private industries are controlled by the industries they regulate because the President has appointed to their boards men from these industries.

As respect for impartial professional experts grows, as government assumes the function of supplying campaign funds, American presidents will appoint more and more social scientists to the boards of these powerful federal agencies. By 2050 nearly all such agencies will be effectively controlled by experts in government, not by politicians and industry representatives. This will be a significant advance towards government by experts.

MORE GOVERNMENT USE OF LEGISLATIVE EXPERTS

Another old trend that is slowly creating government by experts is the ever-increasing use of experts in the legislative process. Elected legislators and executives are employing more and more economists, political scientists, sociologists, anthropologists, and other social scientists to propose and write new legis-

The Transition to Government by Experts

lation and to advise them on laws proposed by other men. This is a well-established trend in every advanced country and it is certain to continue until full government by experts is achieved. By 2100 Congress will employ a staff of expert consultants over ten times as large as the Congress itself. (In 1963 it was only half as large.) Moreover, every major federal and state agency will then employ a staff of social scientists whose sole function will be to review and propose new legislation and new administrative policies. In the last stage of democratic government, all new legislation will be proposed by such experts. Legislatures will merely vote on laws proposed by relatively independent experts, and only on the most important of these. Minor laws proposed by experts will become law without legislative action, by administrative ruling.

THE CENTRALIZATION OF GOVERNMENT

A further established trend that will continue to increase the number and the influence of experts under democratic government is the gradual shift of governmental functions from local to state and national agencies. Because the larger regional and central government agencies use civil service procedures and expert advisors far more extensively and efficiently than most smaller local agencies, this centralization will steadily increase the role of experts in government.

For instance in America, the functions of enacting and enforcing criminal laws, providing judicial services, and caring for convicted criminals will be slowly but surely transferred from local and state governments to the federal government. And the federal government will steadily increase its already relatively advanced reliance on sociologists, criminologists, penologists, and other experts on crime. By 2100 all American criminal laws will be written by such experts, approved by the Congress, and enforced by highly trained experts in police work and penology employed by the national government.

MORE PROFESSIONAL BUSINESS MANAGERS

The last old trend toward government by experts is the transfer of managerial control over large private corporations from private owners to hired professional managers. This trend has long been obvious among very large private corporations like General Motors and American Telephone and Telegraph. It will soon become obvious among medium-sized firms, and eventually among small corporations. It results from the sale or resale of common stock to ever larger numbers of investors, none of whom can individually control any of the enterprises whose stock they own.

When stock has been sufficiently widely distributed, the election of corporation directors becomes as undemocratic as political elections in Communist states. New directors are co-opted by the old board of trustees, which is dominated by whoever controls the collection of proxies, usually the old management. Thus, new corporation presidents are indirectly appointed by the old management. If the old president is a professionally trained manager, he usually chooses a similar replacement, after consultation with his fellow executives, i.e., with professional colleagues.

This is management by experts. It will become government by experts as these firms are taken over by the state if this method of choosing business executives is retained. And, if some other method is adopted, such as that used by the BBC or TVA, the new method will almost certainly be another form of management or government by experts.

New Trends Toward Government by Experts

The trends toward government by experts noted above are all now apparent, indeed have long been apparent. Let us turn now to some that are either much less apparent or non-existent as yet, but that I believe will eventually appear and become obvious.

HIGHER EDUCATIONAL QUALIFICATIONS FOR CANDIDATES

First, I predict that educational restrictions on nomination for public office will be introduced and gradually raised until only university graduates with advanced degrees are eligible for election to public office. Such restrictions are unpopular now because higher education has been largely limited to children of upper-income parents. They will become more politically feasible as higher and professional education become more easily available to the children of low-income parents.

By 2040 all candidates for state legislatures and the United States Congress will have to have a B.A. or M.A. degree, or their equivalent. By 2150 all national legislators in advanced democratic countries will have a Ph.D. degree in social science. This high educational requirement for national legislators will be adopted well before democratic government has been replaced by expert government.

THE RESTRICTION OF LEGISLATIVE WORK

Second, I predict that democratically elected legislatures will soon begin to restrict their activities more and more to the formulation of general policies. Eventually, all new laws enacted in democratic states will be very brief and very broad policy statements. For instance, instead of enacting a tax law containing a hundred thousand words, the Congress will approve a one-page policy statement instructing the treasury to raise income and/or sales taxes enough to bring in specified additional revenues. Instead of enacting a tariff law fixing duties on thousands of individual goods, it will, in a few simple sentences, order the Tariff Commission to fix tariffs high enough to protect essential domestic industries or to raise some specified sum. As a result, the detailed interpretation and administration of laws will be increasingly entrusted to experts.

THE RISE OF PROFESSIONAL JOURNALISTS

A third new major trend creating government by experts will be the gradual rise of professional management of all means of public information—newspapers, magazines, publishing firms, and radio and television stations. The businessmen who now own and/or manage such enterprises will be slowly replaced by professional journalists, editors, and educators. Of course, some professional business managers will always be needed to handle purely business activities—accounting, plant maintenance, and budgeting—but their control over editorial and news policies will be gradually eliminated.

This long-run trend will be greatly promoted by the inevitable socialization of the ownership of all means of public information. By 2150 nearly all such media in democratic countries will be owned by consumers' co-ops, learned societies, and cultural groups—not by national governments—and will be run to inform or influence public opinion, not to make a profit.

Well before their socialization, newspapers in most democratic countries will become regulated, monopolistic public utilities. They will be required to become more and more politically and religiously non-partisan. Their editors will be increasingly freed from influence by private owners, advertisers, political parties, and government officials. Eventually, all chief editors will be chosen by their professional association, not by private owners or government agencies. And all editorials or news stories on political events and social developments will be written by men who are Ph.D.s in modern history or social science, as well as able journalists.

THE RISE OF PROFESSIONAL SCHOOL ADMINISTRATORS

The control of schools and universities by elected or politically appointed administrators, trustees, and school board members—most of whom now are nonprofessionals—will gradually give way to control by professional educators chosen directly or indirectly by their professional associations and/or by their facul-

The Transition to Government by Experts

ties. It is irrational and unscientific to allow the butcher, the baker, and the candlestick maker to choose the men who run schools and universities, or to review textbooks and teaching methods. Only professional educators are qualified to perform such functions.

One of the first major steps in the trend will be to allow teachers and professors to elect one or two members of the boards that govern their schools. Later their representation on these boards will be repeatedly increased, until all members are educators elected by educators, or until such boards are replaced by single administrators chosen by educators.

It will, of course, always be necessary for some higher agency of government to determine annual expenditures for education. Every profession has an exaggerated idea of the importance of its work and would like to have more financial support than it should have. But the use of funds appropriated for education will increasingly be determined by professional educators chosen by educators, not by elected officials.

GOVERNMENT FINANCING OF POLITICAL CAMPAIGNS

The political influence of rich men in democratic states will be gradually reduced, and that of experts gradually increased, by the growth of government financing of political campaigns. It is now very expensive to run for high public office. For instance, a successful candidate for the United States Senate from California must spend over a million dollars if he has serious opposition. And a successful candidate for the Republican or Democratic nomination for the Presidency must spend far more, merely to win the nomination. Therefore, the wealthy men who supply the campaign funds have great influence in determining who will seek and win high political office.

During the next century all advanced countries will gradually adopt the policy of providing ample public funds and/or free and ample publicity for all candidates for public office and prohibiting large private expenditures on political campaigns. This will increasingly restrict the political influence of wealthy men and increase that of all their political rivals, including especially intellectuals and social scientists.

In West Germany governments already provide substantial campaign funds. In 1967, for the first time, the United States Congress seriously considered the provisions of several million dollars for national political campaigns. As the years pass, the provision of such funds will become more and more generous and ample. By 2100 over 90 percent of all campaign costs, local as well as national, will be financed out of public funds.

MORE ADVICE BY PROFESSIONAL ASSOCIATIONS

Finally, professional associations of social scientists—like the American Economics Association—will soon adopt, and thereafter steadily expand, systematic methods of using and increasing their members' influence on public opinion and on legislative and administrative agencies of government. They will begin to poll their members periodically on the leading current political issues in their special fields, and will adopt more and more effective methods of making known the results of these polls, both to voters and to the relevant government officials.

Furthermore, the professional associations will increasingly group and rank their members by specialty and ability—as shown by education and experience—so that their opinion polls of select experts will become more and more reliable indicators of the best professional opinion on each political issue. Such trends will help to prepare professional social science associations for effective participation in government by experts, and will also make democratic governments more efficient.

During the next century all professional and learned associations of social scientists will create special committees to advise government agencies on the appointment of their members to high public office. For instance, the American Economics Association will establish a committee to advise the President on all appointments to his Council of Economic Advisors, and on the policies this council should recommend. To prepare to give such advice, these committees will collect an ever larger mass

The Transition to Government by Experts

of information about the education and experience of the members of their profession and about the consensus of opinion in each branch of their profession. Experience in the performance of such advisory functions will help to prepare social science associations for their eventual role of selecting national legislators when government by experts is achieved.

Before 2000 most democratic governments will begin to subsidize these associations in order, among other things, to enable them to perform these advisory functions. Public expenditures for this purpose will increase both absolutely and relatively until government by experts is adopted.

During the twenty-first century these associations will begin to seek representation in the national legislatures of all advanced democratic countries. After a long campaign, they will be granted some small representation in most such legislatures, almost certainly before 2150. As support for government by experts continues to grow, this representation will expand slowly. By 2300 a majority of the members of the United States Congress and the British Parliament will consist of members chosen by the professional associations of social scientists. By 2400 nearly all members will be so chosen. And if a world government is created in the meantime, as seems highly likely, the same sort of evolution will occur in the selection of the members of the world legislature.

THE TRANSITION IN UNDEMOCRATIC COUNTRIES

I have been predicting some of the major trends that will gradually and peacefully transform democratic government into government by experts. The transition from dictatorship or one-party government to government by experts may be quite different. Some countries that now have dictators will become democratic and then follow the path outlined above from democratic government to government by experts. However, some undemocratic countries, especially those now under Communist rule, may skip the democratic stage in political evolution and pass directly from undemocratic government to government by experts.

In 1940 James Burnham claimed that the U.S.S.R. was already a managerial society. But in 1961 it is still far from achieving government by experts. The top political figures are Communist party bosses, not professionally trained social scientists. It is true, of course, that in Russia, as in America, the number of professional managers and other experts in subordinate but influential positions have been growing steadily. The transition to government by experts has long been under way in both countries, but both have a long way to go to achieve full or even predominant government by experts or professional managers.

Although Communist countries are far from achieving full government by experts, they have achieved public ownership of the means of production, an important, perhaps essential, step toward full government by experts. By eliminating private owners, the socialization of capital goods permits and promotes a much wider use of professional managers. It also reduces conservative political opposition to the introduction of a brain trust at top government levels.

In spite of their historically determined, relatively low real wages, Communist countries have made extraordinary and highly successful efforts to develop free and universal education, to expand scientific research, and to increase vastly the number of professionally trained experts of all classes. Moreover, experts are more respected and more highly paid, relatively, in Communist than in capitalist countries.

Membership in the Communist Party is very carefully controlled by the party. With the ever-growing respect for and influence of experts in Communist states, it seems likely that party membership, and, thus political influence, will be increasingly restricted to managers and other experts. Over a long period, this process could easily achieve government by experts without any revolution or any period of democratic government.

There are, of course, Communist dogmas that may prevent or slow down this development. Every Communist revolution

The Transition to Government by Experts

has been led by middle or upper-class radicals, but Communists believe that Communist states are, or eventually will become, democracies controlled by workers and peasants. Moreover, while Communist governments have strongly supported research and education in the natural and biological sciences, they have grossly neglected scientific research and objective education in the social sciences because they fear that such activities would invalidate their political dogmas.

Nevertheless, as Communist governments become more stable, as Communist countries become richer, and as Communists become better educated, they are sure to become more aware of the very great benefits obtainable from objective, scientific research and education in social science and will require more and more education in social science of all new party members. And, when they do realize the potential gains from government by experts, they will be able to achieve such government more easily and quickly than equally perceptive leaders of democratic states. They will not be subject to an electorate less intelligent than themselves.

8
A Plan of Government by Experts

I hope that my discussion of the transition from democratic and dictatorial government to government by experts has helped to clarify what is meant by the term "government by experts." Now I shall try to make this still clearer by suggesting specific methods of government by experts.

I initially defined "government by experts" as political legislation, administration, and adjudication by experts appointed or elected by fellow experts. Nearly all subordinate executives should be appointed by their superiors, as they now are in a capitalist trust or government department. Government by experts will differ from the final stage of democratic government chiefly in the way the nation's legislators and chief executive are chosen. These men will be chosen by select groups of highly qualified fellow experts, but there are many ways in which this might be done.

The Catholic church is a well-known example of government by experts. The pope is chosen by the College of Cardinals, an elite group of highly educated and experienced fellow experts. The self-governing colleges of Cambridge and Oxford Universities illustrate another method of government by experts. The principal of each college is elected by the fellows of the college, all highly qualified experts personally familiar with the candidates. However, new fellows are elected by the old fellows, not appointed by the chief executive as in the Catholic Church.

THE CHOICE OF LEGISLATORS

I believe that in a nation governed by experts the members of the national legislature will be chosen by learned and pro-

A Plan of Government by Experts

fessional societies, rather than co-opted by old members or appointed by the chief executive. Most legislators will probably be elected by professional associations of social scientists, but this last term will be broadly defined. It will include historians, cultural anthropologists, social psychologists, and all other professions dealing chiefly with social or government problems, in addition to sociologists, political scientists, and political economists. Some legislators may also be chosen by other professional bodies—such as those of educators, lawyers, and public health doctors.

Veblen and the Technocrats implied or asserted that the new society would be governed by engineers. Burnham predicted that it would be government by professional business managers, like those trained at the Harvard Business School. But such men are unqualified to determine broad social, political, and economic policies. They have not studied social theory or problems—eugenics, birth control, crime prevention, education, welfare economics, etc. A government by experts should be largely run by experts in social science, not by engineers, professional business managers, or lawyers.

By 2100 the United States will have well over a hundred thousand professional social scientists, a term I have defined rather broadly. How many of these will participate in the selection of top legislators and executives?

I believe some minimum of practical experience in government, as well as a Ph.D. in a social science, will be required of all expert electors. If the minimum experience is five years, a reasonable prediction, nearly all such electors will be over thirty years of age.

Moreover, it seems likely that the electoral influence of the most able and/or most experienced social scientists will be deliberately multiplied by giving them more than one vote or by a system of unequal indirect election. Perhaps regional or occupational groups of social scientists will elect representatives to serve on a large national electoral college, representatives who must meet much stricter requirements than those who vote for them.

Social scientists differ widely in their preparation to serve as legislators and solve a wide variety of current social problems. Very few are broadly trained and/or experienced. The great majority specialize in some specific, often narrow, field—such as agricultural economics, population theory, juvenile delinquency, or social insurance. An anthropologist who has devoted most of his professional life to studying and teaching about primitive tribes is not well prepared to vote on new tax or insurance laws in an advanced country, or to select those who do so. The same conclusion is valid for historians who have specialized in ancient history, economists who have concentrated on input-output analysis, and other narrow specialists.

A national legislature consisting of such specialists would certainly be more competent to deal with political problems than a legislature consisting of cotton farmers, dentists, civil engineers, and lawyers. *But a legislature made up of general social scientists—men with education and experience in several or many different fields of social science—would be more competent than one consisting of specialists in individual fields.* Because a national legislature enacts laws in all areas of social activity, each legislator should be very broadly trained in social science. Legislative committees can have all the specialized advisors they need, and the members of each legislative committee should specialize in the work of that committee, but each committee member must also have the general knowledge required to enable him to vote wisely on the proposed laws approved by every other committee.

Of course, no one would be more familiar with the relative preparation and abilities of specialists and generalists in social science than their fellow social scientists. Therefore, they would not be likely to elect narrow specialists to positions requiring a broad education and experience. On the other hand, they would have a high opinion of the views of specialists on matters that fall within the limits of their specialty.

The great majority of jobs for social scientists are for specialists, and the degree of specialization required is steadily rising. About the only positions still open to generalists are those as teachers of the basic principles of some particular social science

A Plan of Government by Experts

or as journalists. And the men who now fill these positions often know little about even the elementary principles of other social sciences. *Thus, it will be necessary to make special provisions to train the kind of general social scientists needed to man the legislature of a country practicing government by experts.*

One possible provision would be to require all candidates for the legislature to return to graduate school for one or more years of broadening full-time education in social science before running for the legislature. Another possibility would be to require all legislators to take one or more university courses in social science each semester while serving in the legislature. And each legislator might be required to train one or two apprentices. Other possibilities could be suggested. The major point is that an ample supply of general social scientists must and will be trained.

A social scientist who has devoted his entire professional life to study, writing, and teaching is not well prepared to understand the practical problems of implementing policies and administering government bureaus. Therefore, all expert candidates for the national legislature will be required to have had several years of experience as public administrators. To prepare for such work, they will need some professional training in public administration, as well as in social science. But all such candidates will be primarily trained and experienced in social science rather than in public administration.

Neither business administration nor public administration is a social science. Schools of business and public administration do not teach their students how major social problems should be solved—what taxes should be enacted, whether economic planning is needed, how crime should be minimized, and so forth. Students of business administration learn how to maximize profits, not social welfare. Students of public administration learn only one way to increase social welfare, namely by sound public administration. Therefore, the top administrators of a country practicing government by experts should have two Ph.D.'s, one in public administration and one in general social science. And professional public and business managers who do not have a Ph.D. in social science will not be allowed to participate in the election of members of the national legislature. Of course, by the time government by experts is achieved, all professional men will continue to take university courses throughout their professional life; therefore it will not be unusual or difficult for the more able among them to acquire a second Ph.D. degree.

In democratic countries, provincial and national legislatures include large numbers of lawyers. They made up 48 percent of the United States Congress in 1968. But very few lawyers are social scientists. They are trained to interpret existing laws and to present cases in court, not to solve social or administrative problems by formulating new laws. All proposed laws should be reviewed and rephrased by lawyers, but the function of such review should be to make new laws clear, constitutional, and consistent with other laws, not to alter their major ideas. Thus, under government by experts the national legislature should contain few if any lawyers untrained in social science, and the legal profession should not participate in the selection of social scientists to serve in the legislature. Of course, some social scientists would find supplementary training in certain fields of law useful, and a few might become fully qualified lawyers, but they should serve in the legislature as social scientists.

Although lawyers as such are not social scientists, some law courses and some kinds of legal practice teach lawyers a good deal about certain social theories and problems. Moreover, continuing adult university education will become more and more popular and available in the future. Thus, it should become increasingly feasible for lawyers to do enough adult university work in the social sciences to qualify them for participation as social scientists in government by experts.

Will the social scientists who elect national legislator and chief executives be organized in formal political parties? I think that they will, for the number of men qualified to serve as expert electors in advanced nations will be very large, probably over two hundred thousand in the United States by 2100. It will be very difficult if not impossible for such a large number

A Plan of Government by Experts

of persons to formulate major issues and agree on strong candidates unless they are organized in competing political parties that conduct party conventions and/or primary party elections. Even among social scientists, there will long remain a basic conservative-liberal split, although the range of opinion on each major issue should narrow steadily as the social sciences advance.

Of course, elections are a very poor method of determining public opinion, even among experts. Public opinion polls can perform this function far better than elections. Therefore, political parties and elections will be needed chiefly in order to choose candidates for the national legislature and, perhaps, for the office of chief national executive.

Some critics of democratic government have argued that legislators would be more representative and more competent if they were elected by vocational or industrial groups instead of by regional areas. It is true that a legislator elected by lawyers might be more familiar with their problems, and more eager to support their interests, than one elected by a regional area. But the main result of vocational or industrial representation would be more competent and vigorous support of special interests, whose gains would come primarily at public expense. One of the chief arguments for government by experts is that experts would seek to benefit the nation as a whole, not special interests. Therefore such experts will not represent conflicting special interest. They will be chosen by social scientists because such electors could evaluate the performance of expert rulers more competently than could any other group of electors, not because they would favor the special interests of this small professional group. And effective measures will be adopted to minimize any special favors for this group.

THE FUNCTIONS OF THE NATIONAL LEGISLATURE

Why would a national legislature be needed in a government administered by experts? Could not the expert administrators and their specialized consultants determine their own agency policies more wisely than less specialized and experienced generalists in a separate legislature?

The great merit of such generalists is that they are not biased in favor of any one agency. They can look at proposed laws from the national viewpoint, at least they can do so if they are chosen by the nation or by all qualified electors instead of by local districts. A member of the staff of a subordinate administrative agency, like the representative of an electoral district, is usually parochial or provincial.

The fundamental thesis of this study is that all political decisions should, and therefore eventually will, be made by experts. This thesis implies that under government by experts the national legislature will delegate to subordinate agencies all decisions concerning which these agencies are more expert. It will not tell the armed forces what weapons to use or where to locate military camps and naval bases. Nor will it tell prison officials where or when to build new prisons.

However, there are certain major functions that cannot or should not be delegated to subordinate agencies. For instance, in the absence of a constitution the legislature itself must create and abolish all major agencies of government. And it must assign functions to them and allocate funds among them. But it need not control the internal organization or budget of any subordinate agency because the managers of each agency should be more expert at these tasks, and also have more time and staff to devote to them.

Under government by experts, a national legislature will also be needed to serve as the supreme lawmaker. It will determine the most general national policies, those that affect two or more top government agencies, but will not prescribe any operating rule or policy that a single agency is more competent to determine. For instance, it will assign the function of handling mail to the post office system, but will not determine how this very general function is to be carried out. It will assign the function of providing ideal social insurance to the social insurance agency, but will not prescribe insurance coverage, rates, or payments. All such details will be left to the agency because

A Plan of Government by Experts

its executives and advisors will be more expert in these matters and have more time for them.

The national legislature will control the volume of national saving because saving affects all government agencies and all citizens, but it will not allocate investment funds among alternative uses. This function will be delegated to an investment agency, which will allocate all funds to the highest bidders, by raising and lowering the interest rate. Uneconomic use of such funds by state agencies and trusts will be controlled by removing offending executives, not by controlling individual loans.[1]

The legislature will also prescribe simple general principles of wage and price determination because all agencies and firms should apply the same wage and price rules. Uneconomic price and wage determination will be controlled by instructing, penalizing, and removing the executives responsible, not by prescribing individual prices and wage rates.[2]

Nearly all criminal laws are now enacted by legislatures, but under government by experts the great majority of such laws will be enacted by more specialized and expert agencies. For instance, traffic laws will be written by the agency that builds and maintains streets and highways and/or by national and local police authorities, and/or by the national auto accident insurance agency because these agencies will know much more about highways and auto accidents than any legislature. Similarly, and for the same reason, all detailed health laws will be written by the national health department, all detailed social insurance and pension laws by the national department of social insurance, all such education laws by the department of education, and so forth. Expert legislatures may continue for some time to pass detailed laws which cannot be based upon expert scientific study, such as purely moral or religious laws—on sexual behavior, marriage, divorce, treatment of the flag, suicide, blasphemy, euthanasia and the like—but they will eventually abandon all efforts to enforce moral, religious, and patriotic behavior by law.

Under government by experts the national legislature will determine national population and eugenic policies because such policies affect all voters and arouse strong emotional reactions. Because most methods of implementing general population and eugenic policies also arouse such reactions, the legislature may long retain control over detailed as well as general policies of this kind.

The net result of all the decentralization of legislation predicted above will be at least an eighty percent reduction in the work load of the United States Congress. This will permit it to give far more careful consideration to the basic, general laws it continues to enact. At the same time, this decentralization will greatly increase the need for separate expert policy-determination committees or subordinate legislatures in all large government agencies. These expert agency legislatures or legislative councils will replace the regional and local legislative bodies that now enact so many laws and ordinances in democratic countries.

AGENCY LEGISLATURES

As explained earlier, men trained and experienced in business management or public administration only are not social scientists and are not most competent to determine the social policies of government agencies. Yet I have predicted that, under government by experts, most legislative functions will be delegated by national legislatures to administrative agencies. Indeed, this transfer of functions has long been going on in all democratic countries. How will these agencies assure that their policy decisions are made by the appropriate experts, by social scientists who have specialized in the social problems involved?

First, I predict that the practice of appointing politicians, business executives, and public administrators untrained in social science as agency chiefs will be abandoned. All such executives will be required to have a substantial professional training in the relevant field of social science as well as professional training and experience in public administration.

Second, and much more important, within each major government department the function of policy determination will be separated from that of policy implementation or administration and assigned to a policy committee or agency legislature composed largely or entirely of social scientists who have long specialized in the field of the bureau's activities. These social scientists and their fellow legislators will be freed from all administrative duties, and will also be largely independent of control by the chief executives of their agency.

Such assignment of policy formulation to a separate group of experts is inevitable because: (1) the collective decision of a group is usually wiser than that of a single individual; (2) administrators are too busy to give enough time and thought to policy decisions; and (3) the professional training and experience required for policy determination is quite different from that required for policy administration. In sum, the case for an agency legislature within each large government bureau is as strong as, and very similar to, the case for a separate legislature in each national government.

The membership of agency legislatures will be largely or wholly selected by the entire body of social scientists who are experts in the work of such agencies, not by the administrators of these agencies. Selection by the administrators would make them too responsive to the wishes of a single man, and one who is primarily an administrator, not an expert in policy determination.

Each professional social science association will include sections that contain only members specializing in problems that fall within the scope of a single major government bureau—such as medical care, education, crime, social insurance, taxation, and banking. These sections will include journalists, research workers, and professors as well as civil service employees. All members of the association will take part in the election of the national legislature, but only the members of a single section will participate in the election of an agency legislature.

Agency legislatures will of course be subordinate to national legislatures. They will not be allowed to ignore or alter the general policies approved by the national legislature. But they will have very wide powers to determine how general national policies are applied.

American corporations have long made use of policy-determining committees, whose judgment is better than that of the average executive, but these committees are manned by executives who are usually too busy and too unspecialized to arrive at the best policies. If our analysis is sound, large business corporations, as well as large government agencies, will move steadily towards reliance on ever more independent professionally staffed policy-making internal committees or councils.

THE CHOICE OF THE CHIEF EXECUTIVE

The chief executive of a nation governed by experts might be chosen in any of several ways. All that is essential is that he be an expert chosen by experts in government.

First, he might be chosen by his predecessor from his immediate subordinates, as presidents of most very large corporations now are. The chief objections to this method are that it might facilitate dictatorship or rule by a small clique. The chief advantage is that it would assure selection by a highly competent expert thoroughly familiar with the expert chosen.

Second, he might be chosen by a large group of fellow administrators, for instance, the cabinet of the previous chief executive, from their own ranks. This seems preferable to the first method because it broadens the selecting group. It has much the same advantages, although it is easier to evaluate a subordinate than an associate.

Third, he might be elected by the national legislature. Legislators would be less familiar with his administrative work and record, and less competent judges of such work than his fellow executives. But the legislators might be required to choose among a small number of senior executives, all of whom should be highly competent. And selection by the legislature would reduce the risk of dictatorship and would help to assure the

A Plan of Government by Experts

carrying out of its laws and policies. This method therefore seems the most likely to be chosen.

Fourth, the chief executive might be directly elected, like legislators, by the entire body of social scientists qualified to participate in the selection of legislators, or by senior members of this body. I think this method would prove less efficient than the third because most social scientists would lack the direct personal knowledge of the candidates and the experience in high political office needed to choose wisely among senior candidates for the highest national administrative office. All social scientists are highly qualified to vote on some social policies, and hence for legislators, but few are qualified to judge the administrative competence of senior public executives.

Fifth, the chief executive of a nation might be chosen by the national professional association of public administrators. I have argued that the function of administration is quite different from that of legislation. This argument implies that a chief administrator should be chosen by other administrators, not by legislators. On the other hand, chief executives might still have very important legislative functions—such as proposing new laws and interpreting old laws. As long as they have such legislative functions, the argument that they should be chosen by the legislature or by those who elect legislators will be very plausible. I predict that one of these two methods will be used during the initial period of government by experts, both for this reason and because one or the other is traditional in most democratic countries, but that much later, after the function of administration has been much more sharply separated from that of legislation, the chief executive will be chosen by a large or small body of senior professional public administrators. If chosen by fellow administrators he should be removable by the legislature for failing to implement the laws it enacts.

The qualifications required for membership in national legislatures will be much higher than those required for membership in a professional association of social scientists, and those for election as chief executive will be both higher and different.

A university professor of social science may be well qualified to vote for members of the legislature or to serve on it, but very poorly qualified to serve as a chief executive. All candidates for the office of chief executive should have had several years of experience in very high executive positions, as well as graduate professional training in both public administration and general social science.

THE RETENTION OF DEMOCRATIC RITUAL

In countries once democratic or semi-democratic, the ritual of democratic elections will probably be retained long after nearly all important functions of government have been transferred from legislators and other officials elected by the people to those chosen by fellow experts. In England, Sweden, and other democracies, the ritual of monarchy has long survived government by kings.

The retention of democratic ritual under government by experts will facilitate the peaceful and rapid acceptance of government by experts. A very large number of voters will remain unaware of the fundamental change if the old ritual is preserved. And some alert opponents of the change will be partially reconciled to it by the preservation of the old ritual. All rituals tend to become the object of emotional attachment for many people as they become old and familiar. Thus, many men with modern scientific views are emotionally attached to old religious rituals.

Furthermore, the retention of democratic ritual, especially election campaigns, under government by experts might continue to be both educational and morale-building, without seriously affecting government policies. If nearly all public-opinion-forming agencies are then controlled by social scientists, these experts could largely control the outcome of elections, as the power elite now does. And the authority of elected officials could be drastically reduced by the methods described in previous pages.

Any election campaign is a means of public education, and

A Plan of Government by Experts

such campaigns would be much more educational if public-opinion-forming agencies were controlled by social scientists. Moreover, these campaigns are cathartic because they give critics a chance to express themselves. And they build national morale by making many people feel free, equal, and important. These benefits could be partially achieved by purely ritualistic election campaigns under government by experts.

Finally, it might be wise to maintain indefinitely under government by experts an ultimate democratic executive who would function much as a weak king in a constitutional monarchy, i.e., perform ceremonies and arbitrate between legitimate claimants for the office of chief national executive when routine methods of selection seem to break down. The retention of such a traditional figurehead—in Great Britain or Sweden it might even be the king—would help to legitimize the rule of a legislature and chief executive actually chosen by fellow experts.

If the transformation of democratic government into expert government is peaceful and gradual, as I have predicted, how will historians be able to determine when the old system has given way to the new? This will be a very difficult task for historians, as difficult as that of determining when democratic government or capitalism became dominant, and the retention of democratic ritual long after government by experts has prevailed will complicate the problem. I think the critical point will be passed when the majority of the national legislature are chosen by professional associations rather than by the general public.

9

Conclusion

I have now discussed and described government by experts, the next major stage in political evolution, and the long-run trends toward such government in far greater detail than any previous writer. In the process, I have stated and criticized all of the major, and many of the minor, arguments for and against this political revolution. In this final chapter, I wish only to emphasize a few basic points, to discuss the length of time required to accomplish this great change, and to consider what will follow government by experts.

THE LOGIC OF MY PREDICTION

The most certain and significant part of my thesis is the general prediction that democratic selection of lay or non-expert legislators and chief executives will eventually be almost completely replaced by expert selection of expert rulers. I have also made a variety of predictions concerning how this change will be made and how government by experts will function, but all of these more detailed predictions are less certain and significant than my more general prediction.

The replacement of democratic government by expert government will amount to a political revolution, but it will be a long, gradual, and peaceful revolution. It will result from the slow but steady growth of popular respect for social science and social scientists, and for professionalism and specialization, not from class warfare or the rise of a new social class. Social scientists will never constitute more than an extremely small percentage of the total population. It will be chiefly their growing knowledge, not their growing numbers, that will steadily increase public respect for them.

As the social sciences advance, and as public confidence in social scientists grows, other experts and the average voter will become increasingly aware of the obvious advantages of entrusting the solution of social problems to those who are most competent to solve them. The advantages of entrusting social problems to social scientists are already, or will soon become, as great and obvious as the advantages of entrusting medical problems to medical doctors. This will always be the chief reason for the trend toward government by experts.

As the world becomes more peaceful and prosperous, men will dispute less and less over the division of territory among nations and income among individuals. Rulers will increasingly become experts hired to solve technical problems, rather than authorities needed to rule men. Every increase in national and average personal income will increase the effective freedom of individuals to choose among a wide variety of occupations, home towns, houses, and luxury goods. Each increase will also reduce their resentment against socially desirable rules and regulations and their fear of exploitation by ruling classes and governments. At the same time, the problems of government will become ever more complex. Thus, men will find it increasingly sensible to assign these problems to social scientists and to look on political officials as hired experts rather than as authoritarian rulers.

WHY IT HAS BEEN IGNORED

If this argument is as sound and obvious as I claim it to be, why has it been so long virtually ignored? Why is this probably the first book ever written on government by experts?

One plausible answer is that men of power and property, who largely control the expression of opinion in capitalist states, fear any radical political change as a threat to their vested interests, and therefore discourage all discussion of such changes. But they have been unable to prevent a long-continuing detailed discussion of the rise of socialism, which they surely fear more than the rise of government by experts. Thus, there must be other special reasons for the neglect of the case for government by experts.

As noted earlier, the chief of these special, additional reasons is probably the fact that there is no new rising social class that would benefit, at the expense of an older ruling class, from the adoption of government by experts. The social scientists, who would dominate a government of experts, are not a separate social class. Like doctors of medicine, they can and will serve all social classes as hired experts.

Another important reason is that social science is itself so new and incompletely developed that it has as yet had a very slight effect on public opinion.

HOW LONG WILL THE TRANSITION LAST?

Let us turn now to the problem of how long the transition to government by experts will require.

The terrible danger of one or more devastating nuclear wars is so great that the chief political problem of our age is the formation of a world government able to create and maintain world peace. The solution of this problem may require fifty to a hundred years, and until it is solved no advanced nation is likely to adopt full government by experts. Moreover, as noted earlier, the steady growth of socialism in all advanced countries will probably result in the fairly complete adoption of socialism before 2100. These two great political transformations will require and receive an enormous amount of political attention and effort, leaving relatively less for the achievement of government by experts until both of these more urgent and/or more popular changes have been achieved. Finally, it will probably take another century or two to convince most men that government by experts is preferable to democratic government. For all of these reasons, it is unlikely that government by experts will be substantially adopted before 2200. On the other hand, it is very likely to be largely adopted by the coming world state before 2300.

Conclusion

These predictions are based upon the belief that no nuclear war or wars will stop social evolution, or slow it down by more than fifty years. A major nuclear war is very likely, but I am confident that both sides will restrain their use of nuclear weapons enough to permit at least half their population to survive. And the destruction of half of the population of any country, or even of the world, would not stop social and political progress for long. The surviving population would retain nearly all of the scientific and technological knowledge acquired by mankind in the past, and would soon rebuild its housing and industries. Poland lost 20 percent of its population in World War II and surpassed its prewar national income in less than five years.

The concept of complete government by experts, like the concept of a completely democratic government, is an ideal type or limiting case. Full or complete government by experts will certainly not be achieved by 2300, and may never be reached. But even if it is never attained, the concept will prove as useful as those of political democracy, capitalism, and feudalism, none of which were ever fully achieved. The use of such terms enables us to describe in a phrase the greatest of historical trends, of which the rise of government by experts is, or will be, one. And I believe that advanced nations will come closer to achieving full government by experts than they have come or will ever come to achieving complete capitalism or political democracy because government by experts will endure much longer.

IS GOVERNMENT BY EXPERTS THE ULTIMATE STAGE?

Is government by experts the ultimate stage in political evolution, or merely the next step? One of the major arguments against any existing institution is that further change is inevitable. Will this argument be valid against expert government after it has become firmly established?

It is of course far more difficult to predict two evolutionary stages ahead than to predict one only. For this purpose, current political trends are of little use. But I venture to predict that government by experts, defined in general terms, will actually be the final major stage in political evolution. I cannot conceive of mankind ever rejecting the idea that government should be entrusted to professionally trained and experienced experts in government after expert government has been achieved and has had time to demonstrate its advantages.

There will, however, certainly be an endless process of improvement in government by experts. The methods of choosing candidates for higher degrees in social science, of choosing electors to participate in the election of national legislators, of selecting candidates for the legislature, and of choosing the world chief executive will be changed and improved as long as mankind survives. For instance, intelligence and personality tests will be continually improved, and those who choose national legislators will place more and more reliance upon them. But all such changes will be improvements in the operation of government by experts. I do not believe that after expert government has been largely achieved the function of government will ever again be entrusted to non-experts, to persons untrained in social science, or even to experts selected by non-experts.

Notes

CHAPTER 1

1. For a more detailed statement and justification of this assumption, see my book *The Next 500 Years* (1967), chapter 1.
2. J. B. Bury, *The Idea of Progress* (1932), p. 10.
3. Walter Lippmann, *The Public Philosophy* (1955), p. 39. The other data on voting also come from this source.

CHAPTER 2

1. This discussion of Saint Simon is based on *The New World of Henri Saint Simon* (1956), by Frank Manuel. See pp. 74-75, 156, 186.
2. *The Evolution of Social Democracy*, which was originally published under a pseudonym. It was later incorporated in a larger work, *The Intellectual Worker*, printed in Russian in Geneva in 1905. My account of Machajski's life and theory is based on chapter 5 of *Aspects of Revolt* (1961) by Max Nomad.
3. The original, and more accurate, German title was *Zur Soziologie des Parteiwesens in der Modernen Demokratie*.
4. See Nomad, *op. cit.*, pp. 9-10.
5. S. R. Letwin, "Representation Without Democracy: The Webbs' Constitution," *The Review of Politics* 16 (1944), pp. 352-75.
6. *Ibid.*, pp. 357-58.
7. *Ibid.*, p. 373.
8. *Dialogues in Limbo*, p. 105.
9. Quoted from D. Spitz, *The Liberal Idea of Freedom*, pp. 150-51.
10. *Theory of Legislation*, p. 450; Spitz, *op. cit.*, p. 345.
11. For another illustration of contemporary neglect of the idea of government by experts, see S. S. Wolin's *Politics and Vision, Continuity and Vision in Western Political Thought* (1960).

CHAPTER 3

1. These reports are taken from Stuart Chase, *American Credos* (New York: Harper & Bros., 1962), pp. 109-10.

2. M. Shubik, "Information, Rationality, and Free Choice," *Daedalus* (Summer 1967), pp. 773-74.
3. Quoted from Max Eastman, ed. *Capital and Other Writings by Karl Marx* (Modern Library, 1932), p. 1.
4. *Politics and Vision* (1960), p. 427.
5. For these and other reports on voter apathy, see Chase, *op. cit.*, pp. 106-61.
6. *San Francisco Chronicle*, 2 January 1967, p. 4.
7. J. A. Schumpeter, *Capitalism, Socialism and Democracy* (1942), p. 287.
8. Quoted from Letwin, *op. cit.*, p. 356.
9. I.Q.-improving drugs and man-machine symbiosis were predicted in the Rand Corporation Delphi Experiments in 1963-64. See the *Futurist* (December 1968), pp. 128-29.
10. Alexander Heard, *International Encyclopedia of the Social Sciences* (1967), Vol. XII, p. 240.
11. Peter Odegard, *American Politics*, 2d ed. (1947), p. 704.
12. *The Next 500 Years*, pp. 56-58.

CHAPTER 4

1. *Politics*, book III, chapter 11.
2. *Contrat Social*, IV, 1-2.
3. *Works* (Bowring ed.), X, 495-96. Quoted from E. Halevy, *The Growth of Philosophic Radicalism*, p. 262.
4. Halevy, *op. cit.*, p. 147.
5. *Edinburgh Review*, (January 1809), p. 305. Quoted from Halevy, *op. cit.*, pp. 257-58.
6. *Patterns of Anti-Democratic Thought* (1949), p. 215.

CHAPTER 5

1. ". . . . About Inequality," *Encounter* (London), August 1956, p. 46. See also his *Future of Socialism* (1957), p. 235.
2. *Op. cit.*, p. 115.
3. S. I. Benn and R. S. Peters, *Social Principles and the Democratic State* (1959), p. 343.
4. S. S. Wolin, *Politics and Vision* (1960), p. 427.

CHAPTER 6

1. *The Economic Theory of a Socialist Economy* (1949), pp. 302-8.

2. D. Riesman, "Notes on Meritocracy," *Daedalus* (Summer 1967), p. 898.
3. *Ibid.*, p. 898.
4. *Ibid.*, p. 899.

CHAPTER 8

1. For a fuller discussion, see my *Economic Theory of a Socialist Economy* (1949), pp. 139-47.
2. *Ibid.*, chapters 4 and 15.

Select Annotated Bibliography

(*designates most important)

Beckwith, B. P. *The Next 500 Years, Scientific Prediction of Major Social Trends.* New York: Exposition Press, 1967. Contains four-page (58-62) statement of the theory and prospects of government by experts.

Bellamy, Edward. *Looking Backward.* Boston: D. Appleton and Co., 1888. Often reprinted and translated, this is the most plausible and influential of modern utopias. See pp. 131-34.

Bendix, Reinhard. *Max Weber, An Intellectual Portrait.* Garden City, New York: Doubleday and Co., 1960. Weber described the nature and growth of bureaucracy, one of the major trends leading to government by experts.

Berle, A. A., and Means, G. C. *The Modern Corporation and Private Property.* New York: Commerce Clearing House, Inc., 1932. A brilliant pioneer discussion of the rise of professional managers to the control of large corporations. See p. 22 of my text.

*Burnham, James. *The Managerial Revolution.* Bloomington, Ind.: Indiana University Press, 1941. This predicted the rapid rise of professional business managers to control of the government. See pp. 22-25 of my text.

*_____. *The Machiavellians, Defenders of Freedom.* Chicago: Henry Regnery Co., 1963 (1943). This reviews the elitist political theories of Machiavelli, Mosca, Sorel, Michels, and Pareto. See pp. 14-15 of my text.

Bury, J. B. *The Idea of Progress.* New York: The Macmillan Co., 1932. This is the classic work on the history of the idea of progress.

Crick, Bernard. *In Defense of Politics*, rev. ed. Baltimore: Penguin Books, Inc., 1964. Politics is defined as the reconciliation of conflicting interests by giving them a due share in power. Alternate political systems, including expert government, are criticized. See pp. 114-17 of my text.

Crosland, Anthony. *The Future of Socialism.* New York: The Macmillan Co., 1957. Chapter 10, "Is Equal Opportunity Enough?"

Select Annotated Bibliography 161

States several arguments against meritocracy, which the author repeated in a 1956 article in *Encounter* (London). See pp. 101-2 of my text.

*Eldredge, H. Wentworth. *The Second American Revolution, The Near Collapse of Traditional Democracy*, rev. ed New York: Washington Square Press, 1966. This is one of the few books that rejects democracy and suggests government by experts. See especially chapter 11. See also pp. 28-30 of my text.

Elsner, Henry. *The Technocrats: Prophets of Automation*. Syracuse, N.Y.: Syracuse University Press, 1967.

Friedrich, Carl J. *The New Belief in the Common Man*. Boston: Little, Brown and Co., 1942. This is an orthodox defense of democratic government.

Jordan, Elijah. *Theory of Legislation*. Chicago: The University of Chicago Press, 1952 (1930). See p. 26 of my text.

Letwin, Shirley R. "Representation Without Democracy, The Webbs' Constitution," *Review of Politics* 16 (1954), pp. 352-75. Letwin claims that the Webbs proposed giving too much power to experts.

Loeb, Harold. *Life in a Technocracy, What it Might be Like*. New York: Viking Press, 1933. See chapter 4, "Government," where Loeb argues that political problems should be handled by engineers, not by elected politicians.

*Machajski, Waclaw, see Volski, A., below.

Mannheim, Karl. *Freedom, Power, and Democratic Planning*. London: Oxford University Press, 1950. See p. 166.

———. *Ideology and Utopia*. New York: Harcourt, Brace and Co., 1936. See pp. 188 ff.

Manuel, Frank E. *The New World of Henri Saint Simon*. Cambridge, Mass.: Harvard University Press, 1956. See chapter 16 for Saint Simon's adumbration of the idea of government by experts. See also pp. 12-13 of my text.

Meisel, James H. *The Myth of the Ruling Class, Gaetano Mosca and the "Elite."* This is the first English translation of the final version of *The Theory of the Ruling Class*. Ann Arbor, Mich.: University of Michigan Press, 1958. Mosca taught that the chief function of political theory is to explain how the ruling class is formed. See pp. 13-14 of my text.

*Meynaud, Jean. *Technocracy*. New York: Free Press, 1969. This is a translation of a 1964 book by a French political scientist who uses the term "technocracy" almost as a synonym for government by experts. It reviews relevant French literature and has a good bibliography. Meynaud recognizes the trend toward government by experts but does not approve of it. I discovered his book only after my own had been written.

Michels, Robert. *Political Parties.* London: Eden and Cedar Paul, 1915. Political leaders are, at best, popular oligarchs. See pp. 16-17 of my text.

Mill, John Stuart. *Considerations on Representative Government.* London, 1861. An able early argument for democratic government. See especially chapters 3and 8. See also pp. 81-83 of my text.

*Nomad, Max. *Aspects of Revolt, A Study in Revolutionary Theories and Techniques.* New York: The Noonday Press, 1961. This elaborates the thesis of an earlier book, *Rebels and Renegades* (1932), that the victory of socialism merely puts in office a new ruling class, the socialist bureaucrats.

Riesman, David. "Notes on Meritocracy" *Daedalus,* Summer 1967, pp. 897-908. See pp. 117-20 of my text.

Santayana, George. *Reason in Society.* New York: Charles Scribner's Sons, 1936 (1905). See pp. 25-26, 99-101 of my text.

Schumpeter, Joseph A. *Capitalism, Socialism, and Democracy.* New York: Harper and Bros., 1942. See chapters 21-23. This book contains an able analysis of democracy, but no suggestion of government by experts.

Shaw, Bernard. *Everybody's Political What's What.* New York: Dodd, Mead and Co., 1945. This is far more serious and sound than the title suggests. See pp. 345-53. See also pp. 19-20 of my text.

Skinner, B. F. *Walden Two.* New York: The Macmillan Co., 1948. This charming utopia, describing a small voluntary commune, was written by the famous Harvard psychologist. See pp. 43 and 194.

Spitz, David. *Essays in the Liberal Idea of Freedom.* Tucson: University of Arizona Press, 1964. Chapter 1 deals with "the iron law of oligarchy" and chapter 5 with "the aristocratic theory of George Santayana."

*———. *Patterns of Anti-Democratic Thought; An Analysis and a Criticism, with Special Reference to the American Mind in Recent Times.* New York: The Macmillan Co., 1949. An able Ph.D. thesis.

Veblen, Thorstein. *The Engineers and the Price System.* New York: Harcourt, Brace and World, Inc., 1963 (1921). See the final chapter, "A Memorandum on a Practible Soviet of Technicians."

*Volski, A. (Machajski, W.). *Umstvenni Rabochi* [The intellectual worker]. Geneva, 1905. For a discussion of this work, see Nomad's *Aspects of Revolt*. See also pp. 15-17 of my text.

Webb, Sidney and Beatrice. *A Constitution for the Socialist Commonwealth of Great Britain*. London: Longmans, Green and Co., 1920. The Webbs proposed a notable increase in government use of experts. See pp. 18-19 of my text.

Weldon, T. D. *The Vocabulary of Politics*. Baltimore: Penguin Books, Inc., 1953. This criticizes the use of senseless words in political theory, and also discusses "philosopher kings" (pp. 138-41). See pp. 120-22 of my text.

Wells, H. G. *A Modern Utopia*. London: Thomas Nelson and Sons, Ltd., 1905. A utopia ruled by modern "Samurai." See pp. 70-71 of my text.

Whyte, William H., Jr. *The Organization Man*. New York: Simon and Schuster, Inc., 1956. See especially chapter 3, "Scientism." See also pp. 91-92 of my text.

*Worsthorne, Peregrine. "The New Inequality, More Dangerous than the Old." *Encounter* (London), November 1956, pp. 24-34. This is a sharp attack on meritocracy in general. See pp. 104-8 of my text.

*Young, Michael, *The Rise of Meritocracy, 1870-2033*. London: Thames and Hudson, Ltd., 1958. An ironical account of the rise and fall of meritocracy in England. See pp. 26-28, 108-14 of my text.

Index

Administration
  of cities, 126
  of corporations, 130, 148
  of schools, 54, 132-33, 145
  simplification of, 49-51, 97-98
Aristocracy
  compared with government by experts, 5, 11
  defects of, 58, 79
  defense of, 13-14, 17, 102, 104-7
  as stage in evolution, 5, 11
Aristotle, 11, 75

Bacon, Francis, 12
Benn, S. I., 92
Bentham, J., 76, 78
Berle, A. A., 21-22
Bureaucracy, 8
Burnham, James, 14-17, 66, 136, 139
Bury, J. B., 4

Campaign funds, 7, 44, 55, 66, 85, 88, 133-34
Centralization of government, 129
Chase, Stuart, 157n, 158n
Chief executive, choice of, 8, 21, 138, 142-43, 148-50, 156
City managers, 126
Civil service, 125, 128, 129
Class conflict, 34, 63, 113
Classes, social, 111, 154
Communism, 57, 114-15, 136-37
Complexity of political problems, 46-51, 71, 153
Comte, A., 59, 123
Condorcet, 12
Conformism, 105-6
Corruption, political, 88-89
Crick, B., 114-17
Crosland, C. A. R., 91, 101-2

Democracy, political
  arguments against, 13, 21, 27, 29, 38-49, 69, 84
  arguments for, 12, 74-86
  definition of, 7, 114
  extent of, 6, 12
  future of, 3, 7, 13, 37
Democratic ritual, 150-51
Dictatorship, 5, 7, 23, 56-57, 77

Economics, 9, 34, 47-48, 59, 93, 96, 127
Education
  administration of, 54, 132-33, 145
  democratization of, 27, 50, 61, 65, 71, 108, 114, 131
  elite education, 99-100, 113-14, 140-42
  growth of, 36, 53, 57, 60, 70-72, 108, 136
  influence of, 53, 62, 64, 70, 81, 82, 109
Eldredge, H. W., 28-30
Elites, 8-9, 11, 12-20, 104
Elitists, conservative, 12-15
Elitists, socialist, 15-20
Equality of opportunity, 63-65, 101-3, 114
Ethics, 9, 32-35, 82, 85-88, 91-95, 100, 103, 110-11, 115-16, 123, 145
Eugenics, 42-43, 45, 62-63, 71, 109, 112
Evolution, political, 3-6, 11, 22, 29
Experts
  as advisors, 18-19, 50-51, 128-29, 134-35
  as chief executives, 4, 8, 44-45, 141-42, 148-50

Index

as legislators, 4, 44-45, 131, 139-41
competence of, 42-46, 91-95
definition of, 4, 93, 121
selection of, 44, 45, 119-20, 139-42, 148-50, 156

Fabian socialists, 18-20, 27-28
Fascism, 13, 14, 22, 32, 57
Felicific calculus, 95-96, 115
Free goods, 50, 73, 93
Freedom of press, 106
Freedom, personal, 80-81, 106, 116-17, 153
Friedrich, C. J., 45-46

Girvetz, H. K., 31
Government by experts
arguments against, 14-15, 18-19, 87-124
arguments for, 19, 25-26, 36-74
coming adoption of, 3-4, 36-37, 152-53
definition of, 3-4, 8-9, 138
neglect of idea of, 30-35, 153-54
plan for, 8-9, 28, 138-51
transition to, 124-37, 152-53

Heard, A., 68

Inheritance, 17, 64, 65, 99-101, 107, 109
Interest in politics, 51-54, 63-64, 69, 81

Jordan, E., 26
Journalism, 132

Lawyers, 4, 47, 139, 142
Legislation
agency legislatures, 146-48
choice of legislators, 131, 135, 138-43, 147, 156
functions of, 143-46
functional decentralization of, 126-31, 144-46
geographic centralization of, 129
use of expert advisors, 128-29
use of expert advisors, 128-29
Lenin, 50, 97
Letwin, S. R., 18
Lippmann, W., 38-39, 56, 157n
Loeb, Harold, 20-21

Machajski, W., 15-17
Managerialists, 21-24
Manuel, F., 157n
Marx, K., 5, 23, 49-50, 97, 115
Means, G. C., 21-22
Meisel, J. H., 31
Meritocracy, 8, 9, 18, 26-28, 73, 101-20
Michels, R., 16-17
Mill, James, 79
Mill, John Stuart, 18, 60, 81, 82-83
Mosca, G., 13-14, 88
Myths, political, 14-15, 31

Natural rights, 84-85
Nepotism, 80, 88, 107
Next 500 Years, vii, 70-73
Nomad, M., 16-17, 88, 157n
Nuclear war, 36, 154, 155

Odegard, P., 157n
Oligarchy, iron law of, 16
Pareto, V., 13-14, 88
Personal incomes
equalization of, 63-65, 73, 78, 80-81, 89-90, 107-10, 114
rise of, 51, 71-72, 153
Peters, R. S., 92
Plato, 5, 11, 22
Political bargaining, 55-56
Political goals, 92-96, 118-19
Political parties, 143
Politics, definition of, 114, 121-22
Population growth, 70
Post office, 127, 144
Prediction, methods of, vii-viii
Positivism, 82, 85, 92, 115-16, 123
Price control, 47, 127-28, 145

Professional associations, 44-45, 134-35, 138-39
Progress, idea of, 4, 5
Public opinion control, 19, 23, 41, 90, 132, 150-51
Public opinion surveys, 39-40, 53-54, 90-91, 143

Rationalism, 9, 36
Real, James, 29
Religious dogma, 32, 37, 59, 71, 87, 115, 117-18
Revolution, violent, 23, 77
Riesman, D., 117-20
Rousseau, 75

Saint Simon, 12, 60
Santayana, G., 25-26, 99-101
Schumpeter, J. A., 55
Scientism, 115-16
Science, growth of, 36, 45, 58-62, 70-71
Science, nature of, vii, 9-10, 14-15, 34, 37, 92, 115-16
Shaw, G. B., 19-20, 28
Shubik, M., 48-49
Smith, Adam, 59
Social science, 34, 44-45, 59-60, 121-22, 137
Social scientists, 3-4, 20-21, 24, 27, 34-35, 43-44, 95-96, 106, 139
Social reform, 7, 51-52, 59, 70-73

Social trends, vii, viii, 70-73
Socialism
  effects of, 37, 49-50, 63-66, 72, 101-2, 132, 136
  government under, 15-18, 20-25, 136
  predicted growth of, 5, 22-23, 154
Spitz, D., 41-42, 83-84, 92, 157n
Stankiewitz, W. J., 32

Tariffs, protective, 55-56
Taxation, 47-48, 51, 56, 131
Technocrats, 20-21, 24, 139
Tingsten, H., 31

U.S.S.R., 6, 7, 16, 22, 130, 135-36

Values, *see* Ethics
Veblen, T., 24, 139
Voters, incompetency of, 29, 38-42, 45-49, 69, 84

Wage control, 128, 145
Webb, S. and B., 18-19
Weldon, T. D., 120-22
Welfare, social, 92-96
Wells, H. G., 20
Whyte, W. H., 91-92
Worsthorne, P., 104-8
Wolin, S. S., 50, 97, 157n
World government, 52, 69, 154

Young, Michael, 25-28, 30, 108-14, 117